YOU WERE HERE TODAY

A Daughter's Legacy From the Other Side

MOLLIE M. SWOPE

To Mary,
A most beautiful
and wonderful Mom!
Blessings & love,
Mollie Swope
8/01

PARK PLACE PUBLICATIONS
PACIFIC GROVE, CALIFORNIA

YOU WERE HERE TODAY

A DAUGHTER'S LEGACY
FROM THE OTHER SIDE

Mollie M. Swope

ISBN 1-877809-86-1

Library of Congress Catalog Card Number: 2001086799

Cover Design by Kathrin Blatter:
    cliq
    kathrin@gocliq.com
    www.gocliq.com

First U.S. Edition: March 2001

Order on-line: LegacyPress.net

Printed in the United States of America

10 9 8 7 6 5 4 3

DEDICATION

*To my daughter, Susan (Susie) E. Swope and to my husband, John,
with love, gratitude, and endless admiration.*

Y*ou have everything in you that Buddha has, that Christ has. You've got it all.
But only when you start to acknowledge it is it going to get interesting. Your problem
is you're afraid to acknowledge your own beauty. You're too busy holding on to your own
unworthiness. You'd rather be a schnook sitting before some great man. That fits in more
with who you think you are. Well, enough already. I sit before you and I look and I see
your beauty, even if you don't.*

Ram Dass, *Grist for the Mill*

⋅⟶⟩⟨⊜⟩⟨⟨⋅

The loss of a child is one of life's most impossible experiences. This book was written to honor Susan (Susie) Swope, from birth to her passing at age twenty-two, and her communication from the "other side" still occurring today. Susie's message, "Life is so much bigger than you know and so are you," shines through.

Faced with a major illness, we step out of everyday concerns and confront enormous challenges and growth. It seems we are given partial vision and asked to trust the unknown and the unseen. Learning "here" asks us to look beyond the physical - to be more than we think we are. Cancer and illness bring us not only challenges but also blessings. We can learn our bodies and our spirits are incredible teachers. In a world filled with loss upon loss, we must find our way to healing and meaning.

We celebrate Susie's life with gratitude and awareness of her many blessings. We change and grow, but we do not end.

⋅⟶⟩⟨⊜⟩⟨⟨⋅

ACKNOWLEDGMENTS

More than once a stranger has touched my life and encouraged the writing. Years ago a woman told me, "You will write a book about your daughter and she will help you." I can only accept the wonder of such moments, and feel an unseen support. I thank Susie for all her communications and her love and patience. And I thank John, who always has given his support and love to both of us.

Many thanks (and many hugs) to Patricia Hamilton of Park Place Publications, Pacific Grove, California, who read the (early) book, and called me to say, "The book is about light - Susie was with me." Patricia has been a sensitive taskmaster, skillful editor, and a beacon of hope! I truly thank my sister-in-law, Kathrin Blatter, of Redlands, California, for the beautiful cover design. And I thank Mark Jaroslaw and Sara Stamey for their inspiration and guidance.

I thank Susie's friends for their love and friendship. We embrace each of them as gifts from Susie and are blessed to know them as delightful adults. Several read earlier drafts and helped give me the "heart" to continue. I thank Kathy Kitchens Lyda for contributing her writings (one of her poems inspired the title) and Rachel Roark Glassey, for sharing her dreams and reflections. Kristie Fox, Anne-Marie Lofton, Leslie Miller, Tammy Cook, Melissa Battaglia, and Katie Kenyon all keep in touch and have shared favorite memories, many of which are included in the book.

With heartfelt gratitude I thank all those who gave their encouragement, vision and the gift of their memories: Kathleen Waddell, Carol and Don Kutcher, Eddie Burkhalter, Mary Little, Norm and Norma Williams, Reine Hillis, Jerri Davis, Dorothy Dearman, Mike and Lynn Heilman, Pat and Shelley Curry, Susan Corrado, Bob Kelley, Melissa Miller Gatewood, Virginia Young, Dr. Glen Warner and Helen, Loretta Sweigard, Diana Reardon, Susanne Paulson, Kay A. Clark, Rita Woelk, Hazel Iattoni and family, Franklin Krueger, Dr. Gross, Mary Francis Coslett, Mary Lou Frank, Janice Gauntt, Marie Holmes, George Cline, Samir, Tom Allensworth, Monte Ramme, Lynda Railsback, Donna White, Todd and Kelli Swope, Olive and Jack Swope and the Swope family: Jane Ellis, Polly Truex, Brian, David and Betsy; my parents, Mr. And Mrs. E.S. Kirby, and my sister Susan and brother Stephen. I thank you for your love and support.

I also wish to truly thank Robert Valecka, the Van Til family, Kay Baker, Betty White, Samantha Shoemaker, Michette Shoemaker Fuchs, the Irwins, the Grouts, the Birds, Marc Messina, Darby Langdon, the Klopps and Wolfsons, Katie Schofield Lawson, Tanya Hart, Dr. David Haydon, Ken Moore and family, Audra Johnson, Marcie Radakovich, the Anstetts, Cecily Flavell, Bill Robson and Hiten Patel, Deborah Mallory, Michele Orr, Johanna Gardner, Carol Barbeau, Michele Morgan, Stephen Marafino, Dorothy Dearman, Diane Hill, Susan McDaniels, Mike and Karen Sims, and Karen Ames LeComte.

Blessings and love, Mollie M. Swope

CONTENTS

PART ONE

CHAPTER 1

EACH STEP ON MOVING SAND

That it will never come again is what makes life so sweet.
Emily Dickinson

My daughter, Susie, had always been so healthy, but began having chronic flu-like symptoms in 1986. That year, I took her to three different doctors, but none suspected any real problem. She was nineteen and moving back to the Dallas-Fort Worth area from Seattle, Washington, eager to attend T.C.U. and be "home."

Early one morning, a few weeks before Susie left for Texas, I was jolted awake by a terrifying and vivid dream. I dreamt she had a tumor growing in her belly and it was threatening her life. The image jarred me from sleep, and left me gasping for air with tears running down my face. My husband, John, woke and held me as I quieted.

It was still very early, but I picked up the phone and called my daughter. "Susie," I said, "I had a horrible dream that I couldn't find you. I had to call and hear your voice."

Her sleepy voice answered, "It's all right, Mom. I'm here. Everything is all right. I love you." Susie was amazing in her response to me that early morning, so full of gentleness and love. I was still shaken by the vividness of the dream, but reassured. It was just a dream, a bad dream.

-→∗═○○═∗←-

On a Saturday morning in January, the phone rang in our home in the Pacific Northwest. Susie, now in Texas, complained of having increasing abdominal pain. After a series of phone calls, her friend Rachel drove her to the emergency room. The doctors there thought it might be her appendix.

As Rachel later wrote, *When the doctor said she needed an appendectomy, we tried to 'schedule' it for another time, trying somehow to get out of it. We were really hoping it wasn't her appendix. We should have been hoping it was.*

I called a surgeon, a friend for who Susie often babysat. I asked him if he or someone from his office could examine my daughter. His partner examined her, and told her, "Honey, I sure wish it was your appendix." John and I had been waiting near the phone.

"It's not her appendix. Get down here, we're in deep trouble."

We left on the next available flight.

Susie's friend, Rachel, met us at the airport and drove us to the hospital. I kept saying, "I can't believe this is happening. I can't believe this is happening." John was very quiet. We walked into the hospital lobby, up the elevator, past the nurse's desk, past endless doorways to Susie's room, where she was being prepared for surgery the next day.

The doctors told us an adrenal tumor had spread and grown into her liver. It was very large because it was hemorrhaging and pressing against her ribs, making her abdomen swell. They would have to remove part of her liver and the tumor. The surgery seemed endless, but I will always remember the surgery waiting room filled with friends. So many came to give us their support. Finally we were allowed to see Susie in I.C.U. as she awakened.

The next day, we were there when the doctor examined her. Susie's scar was shocking; it began near the bottom of her left rib cage, curved down her abdomen, and ended on the right side of her back. We clung to the fact that she had made it through. She was recovering and it was over; the scar would heal. We told her it was a battle scar of courage.

❖

The doctors expressed optimism that the tumor was not malignant. Lab results were due back in a couple of days. Susie was soon out of ICU and into a regular room full of flowers and balloons from her friends. She was improving each day, and the doctors said their biggest worry was her lung congestion. Friends came by and visited with her while we left for short periods. I was fighting a terrible throat infection and was exhausted.

John and I spent most days in Susie's room. We left for short periods and waited interminably for the lab results.

On the fifth day, we were still waiting to hear from the labs. We were assured by the doctors that, "99 percent of the time these tumors are benign," but "what if...?" Meanwhile, a second lab had been called in to assist with the diagnosis, which worried us, despite all medical assurances.

That afternoon, John and I faced each other across a restaurant table, shell-shocked from the past week. About halfway through lunch, I was flooded with a knowing and felt as if a shadow had swept through me. My body felt as if I'd been physically hit. I said to John, my voice hoarse, "Oh, God! It's cancer." We stared at each other. I knew, I just knew.

⟶⟩⟨⟶

Exhausted, I lay down at our friend's house while John returned to the hospital to be with Susie. I fell asleep immediately, only to be awakened by the ringing phone. I pulled the receiver to my ear.

John said, "I'm coming to get you. The lab results are back."

I asked, "Is it cancer?"

He answered, "Yes."

I rose and steadied myself, splashed water on my face, and stared into my eyes in the mirror. My body felt jerky and uncoordinated. It was a silent drive back to the hospital. Shaking, concentrating on each clumsy step, we took forever to get to Susie's room. The elevator's noises sounded remote; everything was in slow motion.

Doctors Waddell and Sewell were in Susie's room with another doctor whom they introduced as an oncologist. They began to tell Susie that the tumor was malignant.

"This is an extremely lethal and rare form of cancer. It is called 'adrenal cortical carcinoma.'"

We learned that in the United States there are only a hundred cases a year of this form of cancer, and the only effective treatment was removal of the tumors as they occurred. There was no known cure or effective chemotherapy treatment. If the cancer recurred, the first option would be surgery, and after that, experimental chemotherapy. We stood by Susie's bed as they spoke and felt helpless and terrified. Susie was propped up against the pillows, still in so much pain from surgery. She was silent, eyes looking stunned, tears rolling down her cheeks. She looked at the doctors, then lowered her eyes.

The doctors continued, "We want to operate again, as soon as possible, to remove any tissue that has touched the tumor. This will give you the best possible chance."

They said that they may have gotten it all, and her cancer might never recur, but this would be the best way to insure that.

Time felt suspended, unreal.

I watched my daughter drawing deep breaths, focusing inward, and then to me she seemed changed. She raised her head and seemed to sit taller and assumed an incredible dignity.

She looked at the doctors and said, "Then, let's do it."

Later, I would tell people, "I watched Susie grow up in a moment's time."

—→▭◌◌◄←—

Susie's diagnosis brought our world crashing down.

It was a time of grieving. Over and over, the words "never again" kept running through my mind. Never again would life feel as safe or carefree, never could I *trust* in my daughter's future as I once had. I felt as though I was on moving sand, with nothing solid beneath me.

And resounding through my pain, were the questions: "What is really going on? This does not make sense. Why is this happening to Susie?"

The second surgery happened so soon. Susie was fragile; her abdomen was a giant unhealed zipper. The doctors were very concerned about the congestion in her lungs, and Susie was frequently visited by a respiratory therapist who held a large vibrator to her back, which shook her entire body. She dreaded another surgery and her eyes were full of fear. We were glad when the shots relaxed her into sleep.

I was frightened and sick with worry about the cancer and this surgery. It seemed too much for her to endure, weakened as she was. I prayed in a surgery waiting room filled with friends who had come to support us. I sat, then paced, keenly aware of our friends' presence. At times, it seemed only their loving and caring energy kept us standing. They said there were many groups in Texas, and other states, praying for Susie.

We were finally allowed into the recovery room. We talked to her as she lay under several blankets and slowly tried to wake up. The area over her hand moved; John and I reached under the blankets, found her hands, squeezed, and talked her back to us.

Susie was taken to ICU where she remained for quite a while this time. She was connected to every possible machine, and was kept on a respirator.

After a few days, though unable to talk, Susie wrote questions and messages on a legal pad, "What is going on?" she asked, or would scold us, "Where were you?" "When can I have my next pain medicine?" "Mom, it hurts..."

One day she pulled and pulled on John's watch until he took it off and put it on her left wrist, where it remained until she left ICU. When not asleep, she wanted to keep track of every minute so that she knew when she would receive her pain medication, and if we would arrive when we said we would. We hurried back from lunch one day and found her scribbling on her pad, in huge underlined letters, "YOU'RE LATE!" Although she later had little memory of this period, she was very aware of each and every moment.

She wrote, "Mom, brush my hair," which I would do as often as I could. I put Vaseline on her dry lips and bathed her face and hands, loving the contours of her face. The room seemed labored and strangely alive with all the machine movements and noises. We let a few friends in and she communicated with her eyes and pen.

In ICU, Susie had to endure more than her recovery. One day, while she was sleeping, John and I went downstairs to eat. When we returned, a tall young man was standing over her bed with his arms raised, "Satan has made you sick! I have come to drive the Devil from your body. Jesus wants to save you."

Susie was still on the respirator and could not speak, but her eyes were wide open with shock. We were outraged.

John grabbed the man. "What the hell are you doing here?" The scene was truly bizarre.

The man said he was from a local Pentecostal church. He had heard about Susie and sneaked into ICU to "help save her."

John hauled him out of there while I tried to calm and comfort Susie. The arrogance - imposing his presence and beliefs on her in this way!

There were many challenging moments to those days.

Most of the clergy visiting the hospital were very respectful and kind, but others were confrontational. One Baptist minister was especially persistent. He wanted to know if Susie had been baptized and if she believed in the Lord. She said, "Of course, I do," but that didn't satisfy him.

One morning he quickly stepped in front of me as John and I were walking to the elevator, and insisted, "I want to know your position with the Lord."

I looked at him and said, "The Lord and I are on very good terms." I walked around him to the elevator

One day, I received a tearful call from one of my relatives: "Mollie, has Susie been baptized? You must get her baptized – in case something happens."

Taken aback, I gathered myself together and replied, *I only know…God couldn't love her more.*

Another time, a young doctor not involved with Susie's treatment approached me while she was still in ICU. I was sitting in the waiting room with a friend, feeling overwhelmed and drained. My mind often struggled to follow conversations and my body was bruised from bumping into things.

The doctor said, "You deserve to hear the truth about this cancer. The average survival after diagnosis is six months."

I stood and felt my body shaking. I told him, "We've already been told how bad this cancer is by Susie's doctors," and asked him, "Have you told Susie this?"

He said, "No."

I said slowly, carefully, "You are not to tell my daughter what you just told me. Don't you tell her this. It's not true for her."

Next morning I was waiting for Dr. Sewell to make his rounds and told him about the encounter. He asked me to sit down because I was swaying, and he assured me, "This won't happen again."

I found out much later that Susie had been told this prognosis. Rachel wrote, "She told me at one time that the doctors had told her she had six months to live. I got mad and told her they weren't God and they just didn't know. How dare they tell her that! Sometimes I wonder if I should have reacted that way, or cried with her."

·→►=◉O=◄·

One day I walked into the empty room next to Susie's. Sinking into a chair, I felt that a part of me was physically dying and trying to float away. I did not know how to handle what was happening.

John came in and shut the door. He knelt in front of me and held me. Then he began talking to me, his voice coming from a distance, and in those moments, his love surrounded and held me. Slowly he brought me back with his words and his strength.

I knew I had to change the way I was functioning. One early morning before I went to the hospital, I did. I narrowed my whole focus to the moment. I decided that today was all there was to think about - just today and this moment, nothing more. And today, Susie was living and recovering from major surgery. She was recovering, not dying.

"Look at her," I told myself, "This is all that exists."

That is how I endured much of it, and what was to come. The constant reminders to stay in the present along with John's love and support, and that of our friends, kept me standing many times. I started smiling more and shaking less.

Friends appeared at unexpected times to boost us with their care and support. And I had my knowing that there was much more to this than I could comprehend, my *knowing* that Susie could heal, and my disbelief that she could cease to be.

·→►=◉O=◄·

When Susie was seven, we moved to Decatur, Illinois and she entered second grade. Her "sense of self" was as strong as ever. The two of us were driving to the store one day when she blurted, "Mom, I have to BE somebody. I can't be like you. (Ouch) I have to BE somebody."

I could feel her passion and the greatness in her spirit and I loved her fearlessness. This wondrous daughter of mine could take on the world and yet be devastated by seeing the movie King Kong.

After John's Mom was diagnosed with a reoccurrence of cancer, Susie heard about a bike-a-thon to raise money to fight cancer. We thought she would ride five or ten miles and raise "some" money, but Susie was the only child to end up finishing with the adults. She rode seventy miles… for grandmother. She amazed everyone, received recognition in the newspaper, and thoroughly shook up the people who had signed to support her.

CHAPTER 2

BITTERSWEET DAYS

Sometimes I go about with pity for myself and all the while
Great Winds are carrying me across the sky.
Ojibway Saying

Finally Susie was released to a private room, and our lives took on a new rhythm. It didn't take long for friends to fill her new space with flowers, cards, balloons, and other tributes, but Susie craved something more. She wanted simple pleasures; to have her hair washed, a sponge bath and fresh gowns.

✧⊶═◉◉═⊷✧

So we worked out a system: I would put the "No Visitors" sign on the door and turn the heat on high. Susie would get an extra dose of pain medication and I would move her and her IV poles in front of the sink, and have her sit leaning forward so I could give her a shampoo.

She liked to run her fingers through her hair, and when she was satisfied with my job, I wrapped her head in a towel. Next, I sponge-bathed her, with sweet smelling soap, and dusted her with body powder. Finally I rubbed some mousse in her hair, blew it dry, and used the curling iron. We went through this routine every other day.

Susie hated the way the medicines made her body smell. Our friend Marie kept her supplied with powders and soaps, knowing how she loved them. I bought her some comfortable gowns to wear, and she received more as gifts.

Another friend Janice gave her a cream-colored satin robe with feathers running down the front. Susie was quite a hit the first time she modeled it on the corridor. Her room turned into a laundry, flower shop, and gallery with cards, pictures, and balloons. We hauled in a couple of extra chairs for visitors and more than once John rented a video player and a stack of movies, and Susie always had her cassette player and favorite music.

✧⊶═◉◉═⊷✧

We were blessed to have friends who hung in there with us. We'll always be grateful to the Williams for opening their home to us. We wouldn't see them for days, and could retreat into their cool guestroom with its dark wooden shutters - a safe haven. They were wonderful, just let us be and didn't ask too many questions. We needed that down time away from the "other world" at the hospital.

Mary and Mollie at the hospital.

Another friend, Mary Little, was a daily visitor to the hospital. Beautiful Mary, who dressed in bright silks, wore audacious jewelry, and loved to rattle people with her words. Nothing seemed to faze her; she was a "rock" and Susie's favorite advocate. One evening, we were exhausted, and Mary arbitrarily decided what was best for all of us.

"You go on home," she told us. "I'll stay with Susie tonight." And glancing at the bed, Mary said, "Right, Susie?"

Susie answered with a smile, "Right, Mary."

Mary ended up spending many nights with Susie, and the two of them got on famously. Susie could discuss anything with Mary, and they would talk late into the night. If Susie became sick, Mary would know what to do. Next day, they would giggle about some adventure or mishap the day before.

One evening the "girls" had great fun.

Mary jokingly propositioned one of Susie's doctors while Susie lay in bed with an amused smile, watching the doctor blush and squirm under Mary's flirtatious attention.

Another evening, when Susie was feeling stronger, Mary burst into the room, her fuchsia pink silks flying. "I've had a hell of a day!" she said, and waved a beautifully manicured hand in Susie's direction.

"Susie," she said, "get me something to drink!" So Susie climbed out of bed, walked out to the corridor refrigerator with the help of her IV pole, brought Mary something to drink, and climbed back under the covers to hear about Mary's day.

Melissa Miller, Mollie, Kay Parks, and Kathleen Waddell.

Susie and Mary understood each other. I don't know how we would have gotten through without her wonderful support.

❦

Love just seemed to gather around Susie.

Many an evening, friends or one of her teachers would drop by - or a nurse or therapist - and the room often resounded with laughter. Susie would clutch her small pillows to her abdomen so she wouldn't laugh too hard and hurt herself. "Dad, push on my pillows!" she laughingly demanded.

John would recline partly over her abdomen, his body holding the pillows against her, as they laughed together at the latest silliness.

And so often, she looked impossibly radiant - her hair fresh, eyelashes curled and face glowing with her life force. I was bittersweetly aware that these were the best of moments, occurring in the worst of times.

❦

We learned too, that there were people who could not handle her illness. I remember a friend from my real estate office who came by and was unable to go into Susie's room. She stood in the hall crying, and said to me, "I can't do this. I'm sorry."

I hugged her. "It's all right. It's all right."

Still crying, she left.

There were other incidents. In situations like this, you learn that people do what they can, that the reality of our daughter's cancer triggered grief and fears about all sorts of things - illness, personal mortality and the threat of losing one's own children. John and I learned that that we were a "scary mirror" for a lot of people.

❦

There were also many quiet moments to think about all that was happening.

Tears flowing down her cheeks, Susie would lift her gown and touch her massive scar. Her Dad and I tried to comfort her, and searched without success for the right words. We grieved that we could not make it all go away and give her back her dreams and youth.

Occasionally, frustration and anger would erupt. It was mostly aimed at me, but sometimes at John. One day, after Dr. Sewell heard her snap at me, he pulled me aside and said, "Just remember, Mollie, she's going to be angry, and you're going to be receiving the brunt of it. At times it will seem as if you can't do anything right."

As one of the nurses explained it, "She can vent her fear and anger at you and her Dad, for she knows you'll still be there."

⊷⊷⊷⊶·

Well, I thought, she's still unhappy with at us for leaving Texas and moving to Seattle, so this should really get exciting. Sometimes I would leave when Susie got mad at me, then return in a little while, and everything would be OK. I understood that she was still "youth" enough not to want her parents around constantly, that she felt trapped in bed, in a body that hurt, and that she was full of fears for her future. She had a right to be angry.

We foolishly assumed that Susie would want to come to Seattle and live with us, but that was the last thing she wanted. If anything, she wanted us to move back to Texas. She was determined to live in our rental house in Bedford with her friends; she wanted to get a job as soon as she was able and start college in the fall. She wanted to see her friends, get a tan, and plan a big party at her house. She wanted to go shopping, swimming, and to the movies. We would find out about Susie's strength and determination in dealing with this illness, to maintain control of her life, and to experience relationships and love.

⊷⊷⊷⊶·

Throughout her convalescence, Susie showed her spirit with unflagging humor. She had to be up as much as possible, and we took many short walks with her. One day she headed toward the elevator and said she wanted to go see the babies. Guiding her pole, I walked slowly by her side. We rounded the corner to approach the nursery, a room full of beautiful newborns. It was hard to believe that my daughter may never experience having her own baby.

Susie smiled and enjoyed pointing out certain babies, but I could feel the undercurrents. A woman approached and asked Susie, "Is one of the babies yours?"

Susie made a comment about "giving birth to Bubba," how big Bubba had been, and never did explain about her real condition.

I stood silently by her side. She sometimes referred to her tumor as "Bubba."

A couple of days after her release from the hospital, I took her to lunch and we slowly walked around a small portion of the mall. Suddenly her energy gave out and she sank down, her feet hidden beneath her skirt. She leaned against a wall to gather her strength. Several people walked by, giving us curious but courteous glances. One man, however, stopped and rudely stared.

I was in no mood for such ignorance and said, "She's all right. She only has one leg - and she gets tired of hopping." I glared at him until he hastily moved on.

Susie was quietly giggling. "I can't believe you said that!"

I finally laughed, too. "I can't believe it either. I don't know where it came from."

⋅⟶❯⟵❯◯❮⟶❮⟵⋅

John later wrote, *Susie was blessed with an acute awareness that life is about people and reaching out to others was as natural to her as breathing is to the rest of us. She loved to be around gaiety and positive people — negativity was not within Susie's character. If I were critical of something or someone she would argue the point or defend that person to the limit. It would upset me at times but I cannot help but admire her loyalty. If someone was hurting she was the first to help out with a kind word or a positive hug.*

Celebrating being home from the hospital.

CHAPTER 3

REACHING FOR THE SUN

Inside yourself or outside, you never have to change what you see,
only the way you see it.
Thaddeus Golas

John returned to Seattle and I stayed in Texas until Susie was stronger and able to be independent. I felt so disconnected returning to our home in Bellevue, Washington and going back to work in real estate.

-+>══⊙ ⊙══<+-

In March, 1987, after the first two surgeries, Susie flew up to Seattle for a visit - never was a daughter so good to see. She was tan and golden and beautiful. It seemed that under the adversity there was a glow about her - the glow of an undiminished spirit.

Her scar was still huge on her small body, but she was developing a great attitude about it. I cooked her favorite foods, we visited friends, went to lunch and saw movies.

I shared with Susie that for several years in my twenties I had a recurring dream that my belly was swelling, growing and growing, until I knew it could overwhelm my entire body. Always, during the dream, I heard a quiet voice say, "You can heal. It's of the mind. You can heal."

The dream faded in my memory and was forgotten, only to be forced back into my consciousness after Susie's second surgery, along with a powerful surge of hope. Surely I had been given this dream, this message of hope and healing, for a reason. Susie and I talked about it and she quietly said, "Mom, I know I can heal."

Soon after her arrival, I took her to a New Age bookstore to get some books on the mind/body connection and tapes with healing meditations. As we entered the front door, something happened that I will never forget. Susie walked past a huge amethyst geode about three feet tall. As she passed, her long blond hair lifted and pointed toward the geode, and the hair on her arms stood straight up.

"Mom," she said, swaying, "I feel dizzy," and I guided her to a chair on the other side of the room.

I had read about "energy fields" and crystals, but I had never heard of anything like this. A few minutes later, Susie recovered and asked me to help her approach the geode. Once again, the hair on her head and arms moved in the direction of the amethyst geode, and again she felt dizzy.

Bev, the owner of the book store, saw what happened, and asked her to choose from several crystals. Susie picked up a beautiful clear quartz and held it for awhile. When she passed it to me to hold, the stone felt very hot.

"Susie," I said, "you are incredible." I bought several crystals she wanted, trusting and respecting her instincts.

With the help of meditative tapes by John Simonton, Susie visualized healing and cancer cells being destroyed and she drew comfort from Bernie Siegel's *Love, Medicine & Miracles*. I tried unsuccessfully to interest her in a macrobiotic diet and bought her books on vegetarianism, a diet she had favored since high school. We were on a learning path - not one we ever imagined - knowing there were answers but not knowing where to find them. Susie was becoming more beautiful.

⋯⟩⟦▦⟧ ⟦▦⟧⟨⋯

That spring Susie became involved with Robert, a young man who had recently lost his dad to cancer. We were glad she had a love in her life and that he seemed to genuinely care for her. Summer began and all seemed to be well. We flew down to visit and be with her at her next CATscan. We joyfully celebrated when she passed another big exam with flying colors.

We visited my parents in San Antonio and explored the hill country and Austin with our friend Kandi and her children. We captured the happiness of that trip in a photograph of Susie and John dancing in Gruene, Texas.

She was very excited about starting classes at Texas Christian University in Fort Worth, and in August moved into a two-story house by the campus. She shared the house with three other girls, one of them her high-school friend, Kathy Kitchens. She loved her classes, was happy to be back on track, on campus, and determined to do well with her grades.

Kathy would later write, *We lived in the house for only a year. However, it was to be a year I would never*

forget. The house itself was unremarkable. Hardwood floors, living room, dining room, three bedrooms, two baths, lots of sunlight and one block from campus. Susie found it and we all loved it. How who got what bedroom is not registered anywhere in my memory, but I couldn't imagine the setup any other way.

Susie had the attic, which had been converted into an upstairs bedroom complete with its own bath and skylight. As one ascended the stairs, one felt as though he/she were entering 'Susie's World.' It was always the favorite place to go in the house, and the place where most of my memories of Susie take place. There was always James Taylor or Barbara Streisand playing on the stereo, incense burning pungently, and a sympathetic ear. Her room was the place we all went to when we really needed to talk. This was often, by the way. By the end of a session in 'Susie's World,' things were set right again, at least for the moment.

⇢⇥⊛⇤⇠

Susie's next major checkup was scheduled for mid-fall, but she noticed signs that her cancer was on the move, and our world again came crashing down. The CATscan showed three tumors in her abdomen.

Shaking and praying, we flew to Texas and were met at the airport by Susie and Robert. Susie looked beautiful and more mature. Her huge smile, waving arms, and firm footsteps made us feel we had to be living a mistaken and horrible dream.

We hugged and hugged on her, until she waved us off. "Enough, Parentals!"

I loved watching people respond to Susie. At the airport, people were turning their heads to look at her vivacious beauty. She radiated life. I was so proud of her, I just smiled and tried to remember to breathe.

We went back to her house at TCU, saw her beautifully decorated room, and visited with Kathy and the other roommates.

Meeting us at the airport.

That night, we three wanted to be alone together. We asked her what she wanted for dinner and she replied, "Oysters Rockefeller."

John said, "That's what you will have."

We drove to Vincent's and ordered

Kathy and Marla Morris, a friend.

Mom and Susie before her third surgery. October 1987.

dinner and a bottle of wine. We were all so scared and Susie seemed so emotionally fragile. We re-filled her wineglass that night - and our own. I remember the joy of looking at her, and the heart-break knowing that she had to face cancer and surgery again. Dear God, not again.

It was a foe we didn't know how to fight. We wanted so badly to fix it - to put a giant barrier between it and Susie, anything to avert the danger. We were devastated that she had to go through another major surgery, but hopeful the tumors would be removed and not recur.

John took a picture of Susie and me outside the restaurant. I hugged Susie to me. Our hair was blowing, and our bodies were buffeted by the strong fall wind. I thought, "We are being blown to our destiny."

Susie and John.

Susie slept fitfully that night, dreading the morning. We took her to the hospital early, and again she and I were alone in a hospital room as she changed into a gown. She sat on the bed, the fear obvious in each breath she took, with tears rolling down her cheeks. I held her tightly, but could not get between her and what was happening.

My hugs seemed so little and my intent so big. We waited and waited. An hour dragged by; a few friends dropped in to offer hugs and encouragement. Susie was left in limbo, dreading what was ahead and knowing from the other two surgeries what to expect. John came in and out, checking the schedule, and returning to wrap his arms around her and hold her tightly.

As Susie became more and more anxious, I grew angry. I asked for her to be given a sedative, but we were told she couldn't have one. I reached for one in my purse and gave it to her. A little later, she said she wanted to feel the wind so I

opened the windows and turned on some soothing music. And when she lay on the bed, crying, I cradled her like when she was little. John stroked her head and held her hands, willing her to be strong.

I talked quietly to her, telling her to close her eyes and visualize somewhere else - on a beautiful beach with the ocean rolling in, the sun warming the sand, and the gulls calling. Together we saw her coming through the surgery perfectly, with all of the tumors removed, and her cells healthy and cancer-free. She finally fell asleep.

Soon after, a nurse gave her a shot in preparation for surgery

-->==⊙ ⊙==<--

During Susie's third surgery, the surgeons removed three tumors. They were all malignant. As before, John and I were allowed into the recovery room, and we talked to Susie as she came out of the anesthesia. We kept telling her, "Mom and Dad are here, Susie. It's over. You came through it great."

After a while, Susie moved her right hand with small, impatient movements. The nurse put her hand back on the blanket and told her she was OK, but Susie kept moving it. Then I knew what she wanted: She wanted to know if they had gotten all the cancer.

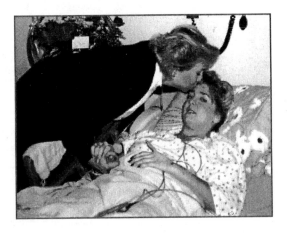

I said, "Susie, they got all the tumors. They got them!"

Her hand stopped struggling, her fingers closed, and her thumb came up. The thumbs up sign! Without words or facial expressions, her relief came through loud and clear.

What a moment! With all my heart I knew there was a way for Susie to beat the odds.

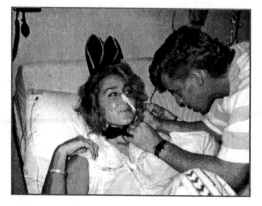

→⊷⊙⊶←

Robert was with her constantly during her recovery. For Halloween, he bought her a bunny costume with ears, a bow necklace, and a bunny tail. Robert put the bunny ears on her head and I pinned the bunny tail to the back of her robe, then fastened the black satin bow. And off they would go as he pushed her two IV poles. Susie was adorable. The patients in other rooms smiled and waved. The two circled the third floor corridor many times, talking and just being together.

Our friend, Mary, dressed up for Halloween as Minnie Pearl, and wore a wig and even a blackened tooth. Susie lay in bed, howling with laughter, as Minnie leaned over her and dangled a treat.

The two of them visited the other patients with John, Robert and I following. Mary would reach into her apron pockets and offer the others a raisin. "Would you like a tick, Honey?" she's say with cackle, and as she placed raisins in their hands they either stared or laughed.

→⊷⊙⊶←

Susie was released from the hospital on a beautiful November day. She was so happy to reclaim her freedom, and to be home among her precious "things.," We picked her up late the next morning, along with Kathy Kitchens, and drove to a park in Fort Worth.

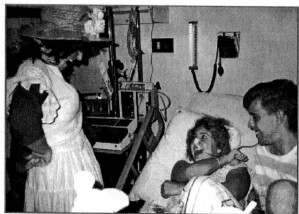

Mary Little as Minnie Pearl visits Susie and Robert.
October 1987.

Kathy took several pictures of the three of us and I took some of Susie alone. I asked her to do something to show how she felt, and she opened her palms and lifted her arms to the sky. I can still see her clearly, standing among tall oak trees, the sun streaming down on her hair and arms, her slim body glowing with light. Susie looked beautiful and elegant, at ease with the world. No one would believe she had just had major surgery and was still bandaged.

Mollie, Susie, and John.

Back in Seattle, we often called her and talked at length on the phone. Sometimes, there was a laughing voice on the other end of the line, telling of her latest adventure. Other times, she shared her bad dreams, or quietly told me how much her body still hurt. She told me her fears and I held her through the phone line, with all my being, loving on her.

She talked about her fears of the cancer coming back, of the painful surgery and tests. She talked about the odds of beating her cancer, and knew they were not good, but she did not accept a dire prognosis. She talked about fighting and conquering it. She feared losing a day's adventure and she feared losing control of her life.

Susie never spoke of death.

The few times I talked about her "not being here," she would say she could not imagine it, and later she thanked me for always believing in her healing and having a future.

Our friend Eddie wrote, *Tell me how things are going. I presume Susie has put on the typical Susie Swope 'spirit and energy' and is looking smashing, bustling around being funny and cute and sunshiny all at once. That's it — sunshine. That word best describes her and her essence.*

Susie and Mollie.

I held Susie close to me when she was a child and was often swept with overwhelming pride and wonder. I loved to see the contours of her face, her expressions, the way her hair would move and lie in wisps on her head. I was pulled to run and experience my own young life, but it was her life that preoccupied me and directed my focus. She was my one constant, and she delighted my soul as I gave to her and gratefully received her love and attention. My child loved me as no one ever had.

In the warm weather I called her "Susie Sunshine," and in winter, "Susie Snowflake." At twenty-three, I distinctly remember looking out over the neighborhood from my apartment window in St. Louis as the snow was gently falling. I hugged my daughter close and felt a flood of happiness in the peace of the moment.

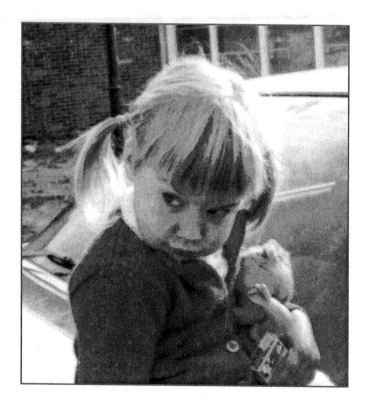

CHAPTER 4

A JOURNEY OF DISCOVERY

There are two ways to live your life. One is as though nothing is a miracle.
The other is as though everything is a miracle.
Albert Einstein

After Susie's third surgery, I returned to our Northwest home, feeling lost and fragmented. I asked and prayed for help in dealing with all this. Within weeks, I met a remarkable woman named Reine Hillis who, after we had talked for awhile, looked at me, and said, "There are no accidents." She invited me to a seminar. The memory of it has faded, but not my inner knowing that my "asking" had been answered. Her presence and friendship gave me strength to open myself to the reality of my world.

That winter, Reine, a gifted hypnotherapist, created a six-week class to explore spirituality. At the end of the class, the group said "We have to continue!" None of us wanted it to end. We met weekly for over four years and still gather several times a year to celebrate our bonds of friendship.

⋅⊹⋙◉◎⋘⊹⋅

In December 1987, Susie flew to Seattle for Christmas, and we played, went to parties, a sleigh ride in the snow, movies, shopping and lunch. All the while, I watched her like a hawk, trying to will her to heal; my energy was entirely focused on her. Although she was ungrounded and restless, we had many great times. Our young friend Katie came over, and we baked and decorated Christmas cookies. We held an Open House and Susie helped to cook and she baked her famous elegant desserts.

I took her to several readings with intuitives, each of whom said how very powerful her spirit was, what an old soul she was, and that healing was possible. They also said that Susie did not come here to experience and learn a lot; that she was a true teacher, and came here to touch many lives; and that "freedom" was very important to her.

⋅⊹⋙◉◎⋘⊹⋅

We flew her up to Seattle again in March 1988. My beautiful daughter glowed, elegant and mature. During that trip I took her to see Reine, who guided her through three past life regressions.

Susie said, "You can stay if you want to, Mom." I sat quietly on the floor and leaned against a wall.

Reine easily regressed Susie to a lifetime in England, when "she" had been a man. Susie's voice assumed a strong English accent, as she (he) described his life and his marriage to a woman he adored - someone Susie knew in this lifetime.

I marveled that I was experiencing this, as Susie described another time, place, and life. Her voice cracked as she voiced (his) deep despair when his young wife died in childbirth, and how he

Reine Hillis

never remarried but was always kind to young ones, for "the boy could have been my child." He lived to be an old man, lonely but serene when death claimed him. It was a life shaped by pain but concluded with a wealth of compassion, empathy, and love.

In another regression, Susie held a position of power, and she spoke of betrayal. Then she began to describe this world, which was not earthly, but another planet with several different-sized moons, dark mountains, and deep bodies of water. "They are as oceans." She identified several people that she knew in this lifetime.

On that planet, she was in a position of great power over life being born. There was a large room where babies were incubated and born, but not from a mother's womb. It was a very deliberate process. Babies were chosen, selected for different talents and functions. She grieved that one infant being, with whom she was deeply connected, could not be given birth/life. She had loved this small being.

Susie next talked of being betrayed by a man at her death. She was drowning in the ocean and reached out to be saved. The man, greedy for power and revenge, watched her perish as he refused to help and she sank beneath the waves.

In the third past-life reading, Susie was a young woman who had a very hard life during medieval times. She described a father who beat and abused her, and a mother who deserted the family. As the eldest child, she tried to take care of the other children, struggling to deal with the rage of this father. (She recognized this man as someone she knew in her current lifetime.) One day he came home angry and hit her on her head with a club-like weapon, so hard that she died. When asked how old she was, Susie answered, "I was sixteen." She cried with the pain and hopelessness she had experienced. Her heart could not understand how he could harm her.

And I, her mother in this lifetime, marveled anew at the hidden connections that may exist between people, the reasons behind experiences and actions that I cannot begin to judge. What other realities below our consciousness are influencing this lifetime? I was being asked once more to push the boundaries of my beliefs and expand my consciousness, fully knowing there are layers of mysteries in life. I believe we are allowed to glimpse only aspects of our soul connection with others, as full knowledge is denied us here.

Reine taped these sessions so that Susie could hear them again, though she seemed to remember them clearly. Afterwards we went downstairs and I took a picture of Susie sitting in a chair. She was a vision of grace and serenity.

An hour before, I had been sitting on the floor, alternately crying or leaning in awe against the wall, knowing I was witnessing something incredibly remarkable. I was on a quest to search for ways to help Susie. In the process, I was learning and growing myself. Beneath my layers of quiet hysteria, I believed in her healing.

⊰⊱

Reine's daughter, Cindy, is a gifted intuitive. During the visits to Seattle, she and Susie had several sessions. Susie always invited me to stay and listen. I heard Cindy tell Susie, "You are such light energy. I have never read for anyone with as much light in them as you."

"You have not spent many lifetimes on earth," she went on. "You have not needed to, to do your learning." She also said, "More than most beings, you must be free."

In her soft voice, she told Susie, "During your second surgery, you were taken and held by angelic beings so you wouldn't leave your body."

I had known in my heart that we were helped through that time by unseen support. I later found a paper on which Susie had shakily written, "Through this trip of life we come to many barriers. Sometimes what we think is a barrier is really a 'friend' getting us ready for the rest of the trip. When we realize this, we don't want to leave the barrier because it has become a close friend."

On another piece of paper with her handwriting: "As we stare off into space, some of us are able to map out our dreams, while others are lost among the stars. Don't let yourself be one of the lost stars."

I took Susie to have her numerology done by J. Spear. He wrote, "Lots of 11's for you. A true master returning to teach the rest of us a few things about life. Thanks for appearing in my life when you did. You are a rare find these days."

He wrote that Susie's destiny was 33, which is a master number and supports unconditional love and balance. Her numerology supported her independence and her humanitarianism. He said her "soul urge" was about constructive freedom. (That word freedom again.) Each door we opened seemed to affirm Susie's powerful spirit - we realized there was much going on.

⊰⊱

We were on a journey of discovery. After Susie's third surgery in October, she had found another special crystal at a rock shop in Dallas. As we walked through the door, she was immediately attracted to a large fluorite crystal, rich with sea green and purple. Intently, she said, "Mom, I really want this," and held on to it. She loved that big crystal and even took it to the hospital a few times. It now sits on my desk in my office. It is a beauty, with the sun shining through the window turning it different shades of green.

·→>|■■→)G■■←<·

Susie sometimes talked about insights gained from a meditation, an intuitive or her dreams. She seemed to gain strength from her experiences and the information she received. She quietly knew she was more than her body and this life and talked about how powerful she sometimes felt and knew she was. She spoke about the past life readings and how she recognized people and their presence in her present life. She agreed that she was fiercely independent and told me that her compassion for all people was growing, though she was bewildered by the pain people could cause one another.

·→>|■■→)G■■←<·

As I was sitting quietly one day, the words came to me:
Life undresses us so we can put on new clothes.

I gained strength through meditation and at times, received blessed moments of peace and clarity in the midst of this crisis. One day, I wrote in my journal: "*At the park, the leaves on the trees were dancing as the morning sunlight streamed through. I felt cleansed and at peace, totally in the now.*

I stood still and imagined myself as one of the trees, with the breeze blowing through me, loving me, and cleansing me. Eyes closed, I allowed myself to feel my breathing and the temperature, to hear the leaves move. I began my day in this awareness and beauty.

In a moment of quiet and solitude, I received communication from an unseen force. I gained insights and understanding. What I saw, heard, even sensed, took on new meaning and dimension. I had stepped out of the ordinary and experienced living in the moment, full of heightened awareness. The two limiting, pervasive elements of humanity — fear and judgment — fell away, if only for a moment. I looked at the thick walls of beliefs and assumptions I had built to structure and protect my life and saw how fragile they were. The words flowed through me, "If the end result of our learning is fear and judgment, is it not time to change the learning?"

CHAPTER 5

THIS EARTHLY DANCE

*Grief is the rope burns left behind when what we have held to
most dearly is pulled out of reach, beyond our grasp.*
Stephen Levine

Our lives rolled back and forth between hope and despair. In January 1988 the CATscan revealed more tumors scattered throughout Susie's abdomen. Surgery was no longer an option; she began an oral chemo that was meant to suppress the cancer.

We flew to Texas to meet with the doctors, and decided to take Susie to Loma Linda Hospital in California. The doctor there emphasized how aggressive and rare this cancer is. He wanted Susie to be part of a protocol to gather information for future patients. We gathered with friends to celebrate Susie's 21st birthday. Her courage and determination were so obvious.

Susie began taking a new drug and the tests showed that it was slowing down the tumor growth. It was supposed to suppress the cancer, not destroy it. They did not know how to destroy her cancer, and none of the doctors seemed interested in working with the immune system. I am shocked at how little was being done with immunology in the eighties, and how much it is emphasized now.

⋆⟫▭⟫ ⟪▭⟫⋆

About this time, a very wise friend wrote me: *When you truly love someone, you can allow them to go on to their own destiny, for you will know that you cannot base your happiness on the presence of others in your life. When you are complete within yourself, you can then allow others to come and go freely from your life without hurt to yourself.*

You must know that people are energy forms, and that energy cannot be destroyed. It can change its form but can never be destroyed.

Your beautiful daughter has brought you pleasure and has served to teach you much. She has chosen her own path, and did so before entering this world. She is a symbol and she is a light that will not go out.

Your association with others, family included, are for your pleasure, but always they must have their freedom. Your lesson is that of letting go and allowing a loved one to seek and learn without strings or controls.

There is something you can do to help. You can replace fear with positive thoughts of love, unconditional love that says, "I'll love you wherever you are for all time."

I felt the truth in her words but rebelled against the unthinkable. I was unwilling to accept anything except my heart's vision.

⋆⟫▭⟫ ⟪▭⟫⋆

John and I again returned to Seattle, after settling Susie in Texas. By now, we'd memorized the airways between Texas and Washington. I would send Susie any information I could find about stimulating the immune system and working with nutrition. I mailed her boxes filled with bottles of vitamins and herbs. She took the supplements, but she liked and trusted her oncologist and put her faith there – and in her strong will.

My heart pounded whenever the phone rang. I was eager to hear Susie's voice, yet quaked inside at the thought of more bad news. She was still living in the house near the TCU campus, with Kathy Kitchen and two other girls. She was determined to go to school, have a relationship with Robert, be with her friends, and remain independent.

◦━◉━◦

For us, money was a constant worry. We had been caught in the real estate collapse in Texas, and in our move to the Northwest we had started over financially. People would say, "If you have your health, money doesn't matter," but it does. It enables you to do simple and special things for someone you love; it enables you to have some peace of mind and not be constantly concerned with financial matters.

Everything seemed to be happening in the space of a few years - with Susie's illness dominating all other concerns. I had many real estate transactions fall apart, and will always be grateful to friends and clients who remained loyal. Our savings account was wiped out while trying to keep Susie in college and pay her medical bills. Our charge account debts climbed with airline tickets and countless other expenses.

Our friends, the Williams, Eddie Burkhalter, Mary Little and Kathleen Waddell, opened their homes to us, so we never worried about lodging. Eddie even let me use her car when she was at home or away on business. "Come on over," she'd say. "I like the company. What do you need?"

During one of Susie's many hospitalizations, I wanted to fly down to Texas but our credit cards were maxed. That afternoon we received in the mail a free round-trip bonus ticket from Continental Airlines! It felt like a small miracle. I left the next day, grateful, and feeling unseen support.

Some of the airline employees at Dallas-Forth Worth Airport would recognize Susie and me in our comings and goings. "How is your daughter doing?" they would ask, knowing my reason for being on the flight. It felt like we had lived on the edge forever, swimming against the current. Small acts of kindness could give me strength for the day.

◦━◉━◦

The phone line between Seattle and Fort Worth burned with our efforts as Susie shared her thoughts, people's reactions to her, her good and bad moments, her belief in her power to heal, her insights and pain, and with a lot of laughter and humor. She revealed her heightened awareness of life with an expanded perspective and compassion.

One day, Susie called me from Fort Worth to say she appreciated her cancer! She said she'd learned so much, and understood things she never would have without this experience. "Mom," she said. "I appreciate my cancer and tumors now. They are a part of who I am. I've learned so much about myself and other people. I've learned things that people never learn in their whole lives."

I sat at the other end of the phone line, listening to these words, and knew that this daughter of mine was on an incredible journey and that I had the honor to be her mother.

People would ask Susie how she was doing, and she would say, "Great!" If probed further, sometimes she smiled at them, "Most of me is just fine" or "Most of me is absolutely healthy."

I believe she responded that way because she felt she was so much more than her body and she did not pay a whole lot of attention to her body. Her scar remained big and dramatic looking, but with typical Susie flair, she made it part of her persona. One day, she had friends decorate it. Along its length, they painted a green vine with leaves and flowers. She phoned to tell us about it, her voice brimming with excitement and laughter. I loved to hear her voice, always full of life, whether happy or sad.

One evening, she called us, "Guess what happened today?"

She told how she was stopped on Airport Freeway for speeding. The police officer noticed bruises and needle marks on her bare arms and accused her of being on drugs. "I told him several times I do not do drugs, that I had had cancer surgery." The way she looked when I last saw her, healthy and golden, I can understand why he was skeptical.

Laughingly, she told us she finally got out of her car, hitched up her blouse, and lowered her shorts enough to give him a good look at her big scar (as cars whizzed by and drivers craned their necks to see). The officer just stared and then apologized for not believing her.

"Mom, I told him he should believe young people." At any rate, she did not get a ticket for speeding.

For the beautiful young person who has touched my soul.
I send love and affection forever more.
The future is clear and the way shines bright.
My love is forever and always, not simply this night.

A Valentine composed by John

CHAPTER 6

HER ANGER

This is what binds all people and all creation together–the gratuity of the gift of being.
Matthew Fox

The chemo drug Susie was taking slowly made her disoriented and moody, her memory and once-sharp mind disguised. She lost weight. Susie was where she wanted to be, and had good and bad days. On the bad days, she needed help going up the stairs. We begged and pleaded with her to come to Seattle, and even tried bribery. Her independence, her love and friends, were in Texas. She would say, "I'll call when I need you to come."

Even as the drug was increased to a higher level to suppress the cancer, it was destroying Susie's perspective and physical balance. Her frustration and anger increased, and with the extreme hormonal crisis, she was in constant imbalance. Her increasing dependence on her close friends - and her frustration and ragged emotions - exhausted everyone.

She and Robert reminded me of Romeo and Juliet, the young couple who bonded together to create their own world and rejected all others. They were committed to each other, but were desperate and scared and caught up in the drama of it.

Susie's anger burst out in criticism of her Dad and me to other people. Then she fanned the flames, which both grieved and amused me. I wouldn't know what to do with a child who didn't have passion in her soul, but this hostile side of Susie was bewildering. When a young child is ill, you can care for them, give them medicine, bring them food, mother them with all your heart. But what do you do with a young adult who is caught between childhood and maturity?

Kathy wrote of this time: *Your passage about her anger struck a special chord, as many of us shared her anger, not at people (although often 'people' felt the brunt of it) but at what became IT. I wrote a poem (imagine that) about it....*

WHAT I THOUGHT
I always thought that those
Who knew their Time Here was coming to an End
Surrendered
Celebrated
Released
And so on...
But you mustn't be so near.

You hardly act the part of a saintly soul soon to leave
Anger
Anger
Anger
And so on...
At least that's what I thought.
Kathy Kitchens Lyda

◆

I had such pain in my heart remembering when Susie would make choices that I felt were not healing. I wanted to tear a mountain down: I knew so strongly that she could heal. I had the anger of the ages in me as my daughter walked closer and closer to the edge. I knew on some level an unthinkable choice was being made. I fought against it with all my resources as I fought, too, to handle it. I would challenge her and myself: "It's growing time." Then I would ask, "How can I help, Susie?"

◆

I had flown to Texas for Susie's latest hospitalization, arriving with the sky thundering and full of lightning - perfect weather for the storm that awaited. I knew Susie would fight us trying to "take charge" and I arrived to confront a very defensive 21-year-old. My heart and eyes thrilled to see her, and I longed to hold her, but she was as prickly as a cactus. She lay in bed, an IV in her arm, and glared at me.

"I am not moving back to Seattle, Mom," she said. "And don't touch my things."

I was tired. "Let's talk about it tomorrow." I left her in Robert's care and stayed with a friend. The next morning I stood by her bed.

"Susie, you are stuck with us as parents," I said, "and we want to help you do what you want. But this is not working. You have to come home with us for a while and get better."

Robert, dark circles under his eyes, lashed out at me, "You don't know what your friends are saying about you. They don't respect you."

Susie was silent and let him say that to me. Both of them looked exhausted.

I think I said something profound like, "Robert, don't mess with me..."

I walked out, got into my rental car, bought a six-pack of beer, and drove to the Williams' house. It was a hot, muggy, buggy Texas day as I sank down in the grass. I drank several beers and had a huge cry; I felt a mess and a failure.

John called that night, before flying down, and I told him what I was dealing with between Susie and Robert. He was furious.

The big confrontation came at the Van Tils' house (the friends we named "Susie's Texas parents"). John grabbed Susie's boyfriend, slammed him against a door, and said, "Enough!" (plus a few other things). Everybody was aghast. Susie, adamant that she wouldn't leave Texas, wobbled off down the street with Robert in pursuit.

What a mess.

Things finally calmed down, and we and our friends talked to Susie. Bob Van Til told her that as a parent he wouldn't have put up with what we had. That startled her. We told her she was coming to Seattle; it was no longer a choice. She was simply no longer able to live on her own.

It was an angry, scared and disoriented young woman who boarded the plane. She refused to sit with us, but thankfully, there were plenty of empty seats. She found a place and burrowed beneath some blankets. By the time we arrived in Seattle, each of us was feeling bruised and battered.

·→·›==·◉·==·‹·

In "A Gradual Awakening," Stephen Levine wrote, *Letting go allows us to flow, to become the whole circle. To hold to any point is to lose our original nature because there is no place we begin and nowhere we end.*

I was ultimately forced to surrender my will in my daughter's transition, to support and release her to her path. How best could I love and support my daughter now? In my journal I wrote, "True support is not seeing our own faces when we are trying to help another."

Where does personal power come from? "Mom," Susie said to me, "I feel big inside…as if I could do and be anything I wanted. Anything."

I knew freedom was part of her soul's path, but what did it all mean? During the last year of her illness, when I felt I had to "get out of her way," I would pray and meditate and mentally tell her I supported her in whatever her choices were. "I will to will thy will." I knew I was being asked to love unconditionally, and that meant releasing her.

I visualized the cords that connected us being released and setting her free. "Susie," I mentally talked to her, "Susie, I love you and support you in your choices, in your life path." Not my choices, for my heart and body were frantic for her to stay and be healed. But I felt I was being asked to free her from my wants and grief. I surrendered, feeling like I had been driven to the wall, but knowing on some level that everything was all right.

One unforgettable day I was meditating, surrendering "my stuff" and sending my love and support to surround her.

After awhile, Susie called me from Fort Worth and asked, "Mom, what are you doing?"

I replied, "I've been meditating and sending you love and support."

She said, "I thought so." She went on to say how she had felt a sense of lightness, had felt very loved… and she knew it was coming from me. She thanked me for loving her. Again, I was in awe of this universe.

CHAPTER 7

IT TAKES COURAGE TO LIVE

Exhaust your words, empty your thoughts,
For then you may come to recognize this one Essence.
Dai O. Kokushi

I constantly tried to focus on the moment.

The future was so uncertain, and the past full of memories. Only in this "now," was I safe. Today was all I could think about, just today and this moment, nothing more. And today, Susie was living and recovering, not dying....

Susie settled in and her anger dissipated as she surrendered herself to our attention and care. We plied her with nourishing food. She gradually regained a lot of her strength and some weight, and began to do things with us. We went to a couple of summer festivals and had picnics in the mountains. Kandi and her cousin, Mary Lou, flew up and helped us with their support and presence.

Susie was invited twice to take part in the "Duck Dodge" on Lake Union. We stayed on a dock and watched the boats through our binoculars. When one of the men on Susie's boat fell and hurt his ankle, she told us she pulled out her extensive pill collection and said, "Here, take this." It was evident in the way he looked as they docked, that she had shared something potent.

One evening we had a wonderful time at a dinner party in Seattle. We played croquet first, then sat around the dinner table and visited with our friends. On the way home, a full moon shone on Lake Washington, illuminating Mount Rainier and creating a magical moment as the lake shimmered with light. We were so moved by the beauty of it all.

During this period, it was very hard to see Susie at the table, often disoriented and confused, and unable to remember things because of the drugs. Every day I fixed fruit drinks with nutrients and protein mixes. We also tried a lot of vegetarian meals. She seemed to do well on these. But I remember being restless, pacing inside, wanting to help turn the tide, to help, and not believe that things could not get better. We took her to an oncologist whom she did not like at all - he had nothing new to try or say.

Susie loved to be with her Dad, and they even had a few date nights. Other times, she and I went to a lot of movies and lunches and had many good talks. Yet she seemed to have her ear to another whisper in the air and she yearned to return to Texas that fall.

She and I were weaning ourselves from our earthly bond – we were letting go; a mother letting go of her child, and a child demanding that she be free. I tried to listen to the inner voice that told me to give her that freedom - yet my earthly eyes could only see that her body was experiencing and accepting torture. I felt the yin and yang, the polarity of our world, hope and despair - judgment and fear versus love and acceptance.

Susie thoughtfully told me one day, *Mom, this is a big classroom in the sky.*

The day the doctor called and said the "suppression" drug was no longer working, I sat at the kitchen table and shook like a leaf, unable to speak. I wanted to fold myself slowly into the earth. I hold a memory of our friend Pat, standing nearby, his eyes filled with compassion.

Later, Kathy would write, *"Susie's way of handling the reality of cancer was to face it head on and with humor. This, of course, forced those of us who were around her to also deal with the reality of cancer head on. She left us no choice. Many of us would flee the reality. Some would try only to run again. Rarely did Susie expose the vulnerable side of her fight.*

The day that she found out she was officially out of remission is forever etched in my heart. It was one of the few days her fear ripped through. The news was delivered over the phone, in the middle of a sunny afternoon, by a health care professional who had perhaps delivered this type of news too often and had lost ability to translate its ramifications...."

Susie's doctors said the only medical option left was experimental chemo.

John and I flew to Dallas and met the new oncologist who recommended our next course of action. Susie and I drove to his office for a meeting but could not find a parking spot. I finally parked in front of the building, in a "yellow" zone, and a man yelled at us,

"Hey, you can't park there!"

I started to move the car, but Susie yelled back,

"I have cancer and I can park where I want to!" That quieted him instantly.

I looked at her. Well...yeah!

The decision was made to undergo experimental chemotherapy treatment. That October, for the first time, Susie was on a cancer ward. It was very different. The building itself felt imposing, the halls and rooms intimidating. Again she was to be hospitalized over Halloween, and we made sure to bring a lot of her stuff along, including her bunny costume and night-light. She would have a private room. There was also a folding bed for me.

The treatment was to begin with a procedure that would insert a tube in her so that chemo could drip continuously on the tumors. Susie was to be given local anesthesia for the procedure. She was terribly afraid and also distressed that the staff wouldn't allow her to be comforted by listening to her music cassettes with a set of earphones.

As we hugged and kissed, the big swinging doors swung wide. As she was pushed down a long hall on a gurney, she turned to look back at us through the window, her eyes huge and pleading.

I couldn't stand it. I burst through the doors and ran after her.

"Let her have her music!" I demanded. "Wrap the cassette in plastic, if you have to, but she must have her music!"

Susie was crying, and looking like a frightened child. I was crying too. They finally agreed to my demand, and I put the earphones on her and turned on her music. I whispered into her ear, "Try to let your mind take you away, Susie. Go somewhere else while they do this." They disappeared through the next set of doors.

Sometime later, she was finally wheeled back out, and we followed her to her room. Suddenly a tall nun, in full habit, entered and started examining Susie. Susie and I made eyes at each other and raised our eyebrows. Already in a time warp, I thought to myself, "Isn't this a Baptist hospital?"

Then I remembered it was Halloween, and many of the nurses were in costume. The "nun" introduced herself and told Susie she was a pretty sick girl, but they were going to try and help her. She looked down at Susie.

"Your Mom will need to buy you a wig, Honey. You're going to lose your hair."

"Yes, I'll do that," I said. "I'll buy you a beautiful —"

"No," Susie quietly interrupted. "I will not need a wig. I am not going to lose my hair."

"I'm sorry," insisted the nurse, "but you are going to lose your hair."

Susie quietly repeated "No, I am not going to lose my hair."

She brushed the nurse's protest aside as if it were a gnat. In fact, Susie did lose some of her hair when she brushed it, but most of it stayed on her head, exactly as she intended.

◦→▸▱▱◉ ◉▱▱◂←◦

That night began a long stretch of days and nights, with Susie horribly nauseated, throwing up again and again. They brought food trays into the room, but she could not bear the smell. The only way Susie could lift up without pain was for me to hold my arm horizontally in front of her, so she could hook her right arm under it and lift herself up, while my other arm then supported her back. I would hold her steady as she was sick. Often I just sat behind her and held her.

The doctors tried many different things to reduce her nausea. Once, after I pleaded, "Help her sleep through this!" they gave her a shot for sleep. Day after day of this existence dragged on. Another time, I was so overwhelmed, I called Reine in Seattle, and said, "Please...just...talk to me."

Clutching the phone, I listened as my friend quietly spoke.

"Mollie," she said, "On some level everything is all right and Susie knows that. Susie is powerful and knows she is so much more than her body." Her healing presence reached across the miles into my heart and lifted my spirit. As she talked, she brought me back to a place within myself that could hold truths, honor my daughter's path, and enlarge my vision beyond the hospital walls.

⇥⇥⇥·◉·⇤⇤⇤

Susie voiced her longing to be outside in the sun, but it was just not possible. The concern remained about her lungs, so I had to get her up several times a day to walk around the corridor. After quite a few days of this, she was exhausted, but had to keep going. One time, after I got her as far as the open doorway to the hall, she went down - a small figure kneeling on her legs and arms. I couldn't lift her without causing her great pain.

"I'm here, Susie." I knelt close beside her on the floor

She whispered, "I can't do it, Mom."

I told her, "I'll stay down here with you, until you can." After a few minutes, I said, "I tell you what, why don't we howl?"

She and I made a few puny howling sounds. We were there for several minutes, while people walked past, some asked if we needed any help.

Then, marshalling her energy, Susie slowly began moving, her face straining as she rose. I helped her up and she toddled down the corridor, swaying and holding onto the railing and to me, as I guided her IV pole. During these walks she would call on great reserves of determination. Another time, on the far side of the corridor, she sank down as she had in the mall after her first surgeries.

A nurse hurried toward us. "Do you need help?"

I looked at Susie, thanked the nurse, then said, "No, she just has one leg and gets tired of hopping."

The nurse gave me a strange look, but I saw a small smile on Susie's face, so it was worth it.

A friend wrote, "I stood in awe when I visited you two in the hospital. I've never seen such strength and courage from within a person. She has set an example for us all."

⇥⇥⇥·◉·⇤⇤⇤

The nights were long, and Susie often moaned in her sleep. Once, about two a.m., we were both awake, and she began talking about what healing and hospitals would be like in the future. "Mom," she said, "it will be very different."

"How Susie? How will it be different? Tell me what you see."

She described chambers of various sizes, where people could sit or lie down, while their bodies were bathed with energies, frequencies, sounds and colors. Every community would have such places, which would be used more for maintaining health than for healing sick bodies.

She talked about "light and vibrational" healing that balanced the body, of healing that worked with the body and did not create pain or place poisons into the body. She said, "Chemo will not exist." Some chambers would be lined with crystals or metals for energy vibrations, others would be lined with colors. People would be welcome to come and go, attuned to their own bodies. Hospitals as we know them would cease to exist. Instant healing would be regarded as normal.

That night I knew again I was in the presence of something extraordinary. I tried to comprehend everything that was happening as I looked at the awesome being who was my daughter.

"People cannot imagine what is coming." She finally slept.

I lay awake and thought, "My Susie! I never thought you and I would have such a conversation." I had really planned on a much more ordinary life.

·→·⊨◇⊫·←·

About one week into the treatment, I glanced – then stared - at Susie: she seemed to glow. She was like a candle that strongly, clearly glowed - luminescent, incandescent. Her body was going through physical torture, yet there was a part of Susie that was lit up. We could all see the glow. One nurse remarked, "She is very beautiful. She has a light within her."

Other times I just stared to memorize forever these moments and the beautiful light she radiated. Her face and mouth had a serenity and wisdom that moved me deeply. The bright light radiated from Susie for several days before it subsided.

·→·⊨◇⊫·←·

One day a nurse from downstairs, who had heard about Susie, came up with a group of medical friends to ask Susie if they could pray for her. Susie smiled and said, "Yes." I joined in and we surrounded her bed, praying silently for ten or fifteen minutes. Susie kept her eyes closed and seemed to bask in the focused energy and intentions.

At the end, a nurse came to me and said, "She will heal - that is what I received. Your daughter is so beautiful. We visit many patients and she is very, very special." Oh, the hope along the way that kept me going.

⊰⊱

I am convinced that unconditional love is the most powerful known stimulant of the immune system. The truth is love heals. Dr. Bernie Siegel, "Love, Medicine and Miracles"

It was wonderful to see the added energy and the color in Susie's cheeks, after that prayer session. She looked and felt noticeably better, she was able to eat and walk more easily. The group came back a few more times and prayed while Susie lay quietly in her bed, appreciating their gift. Her few words, gestures, and smiles spoke volumes.

⊰⊱

I believe in healing, the power of the mind and the human spirit. I believe my prayers are heard and that tremendous love surrounds us in this world. I am without answers or even questions. I am simply here, filled with hope that my prayers are granted: let there be healing. Let the power that I have glimpsed in my life focus on healing my daughter. I am immensely proud to be her mother. Look – her light is so bright.

⊰⊱

Sometimes at the hospital, I was swept up with a feeling of power, of knowing I could accomplish absolutely anything and conquer all doubt. I would feel lifted, fearless and able to visualize without limitations. I savored this visitation of spirit, this gift that arrived like a soft breeze as I sat with my daughter. It was as if I was inhaling a different air and was savoring an expansive and abundant vision of our lives. I never knew when this sensation would come and only experienced it when I was alone with her. I have always been amazed that in this place of despair, my spirit could soar so. All was possible, even my daughter's healing.

⊰⊱

In October 1988, my friend, Patricia, sent a note: "It is fascinating to me, an 'outsider,' to see how passionately Susie decides to live her life. I know and understand how you must see so much of the difficult part of Susie's decisions, but you must admit, she certainly chooses flair and passion as the mode of operation. And good for her!"

I told Susie we regretted she had not had four years of college to experience the freedom and time away from parents as so many of her friends had. She was moving into adulthood, caught in the emotions of a transition between two worlds, and all the while going through the physical and emotional equivalent of menopause.

The two years after her high school graduation had been frustrating: our move to Seattle, her delay in being admitted to the University, her ill health the year before her diagnosis, and then the diagnosis when she was barely twenty. We had not had the time nor the space for her to make a smooth transition from teenager to young adult.

I teased her, "Susie, let's NOT do this. Let's go do something else."

Very early one morning, we quietly talked as we lay in our beds.

"Susie," I said, "sometimes it takes courage to be your mom."

"Mom," she said quietly, "*it takes courage to live.*"

My thoughts float between so many times and places. How can I understand where the future is pulling me or fully grasp the beauty of special moments that feel like small miracles? My vision is enlarged with truths but my heart refutes, totally unwilling to comprehend this reality. I take refuge in reserves of determination, hers and mine – willing myself to focus on hope and healing. Who is this awesome being who speaks of truths and courage and glows from within? I recognize that she is my teacher, facing her reality head on, while I seek to hide from the unthinkable.

Home after chemo at Baylor Hospital.
Fall 1988.

CHAPTER 8

EACH STEP ON MOVING SAND

That it will never come again is what makes life so sweet.
Emily Dickinson

Susie flew up to Seattle for Christmas, laughing as she introduced us to two handsome young men who escorted her off the plane.

I asked her, "Did we have fun on the plane?"

"Oh yes!"

An intuitive predicted that December, 1988, would be a turning point for Susie, and it was, for she was filled with peace and sense of knowing. She was obviously in "another place." I prayed that it was time for a miracle and that her peace would open doors to healing. The dream message I had received long ago still haunted me: "You can heal. It's of the mind."

After Christmas, Susie went back to Texas and spent that time visiting with special friends, going to movies, and being with Robert, who was beginning to falter under the strain. He was so young and in countless ways had been wonderful to Susie.

Now it was January, and there was more bad news: The tumor had begun to reassert itself, and Susie's abdomen had begun to swell again.

"Mom, Dad," she said, "I'm ready to come home."

We flew to Texas, shaking inside and yet so grateful we would have her with us. Susie was in the hospital again, on the third floor with Pat and Ann, two of her beloved nurses. She looked thin, but so pretty with her golden hair and graceful gestures.

I had called my ex mother-in-law, who was shocked and saddened to hear that Susie was very sick with cancer. I wanted her to have the chance to come and see Susie, and asked her also to have my ex call me. I told him about Susie, and that we were taking her back to Seattle. With Susie's permission, I invited him and his mother to visit, aware it would be a gift to them.

They arrived at the hospital early, as Susie was waking up and not yet ready for the day with her hair and makeup. She always maintained her standards of grooming. "Mom...." Susie said.

I stood in front of her and asked them to return in thirty minutes. I helped her bathe and dress. We visited then, feeling awkward after so many years and in such an unusual situation, but at peace with the past.

She looked at her birth father and said, "I want to be alone with him."

I wasn't expecting that, but we left for the waiting room. In a little while, my ex came out looking rather dazed. He told us how impressed he was with her dignity and her "considerable presence," as she had taken charge of their meeting. He apologized to her for the past. He looked at me and said, "She's extraordinary," and I knew he was in awe. He later told us, "You have done a fantastic job raising her - both of you. You deserve to be very proud."

⟶⟨⟩⟨⟩⟵

After a wonderful party her friends threw to celebrate her 22nd birthday, we were finally on the plane, bringing Susie to her Northwest home. We arrived to a snowfall, which delighted her and made her laugh:

"Look Dad, Mom! Snow!" She sat on the couch looking out the windows and talked about making "angels" in the snow, remembering those times when it snowed in Texas or in the Midwest and she would lie in the snow and move her arms up and down to make angel wings.

Now we could pamper her. She complained of being cold, so I ran out and bought flannel sheets for her bed, and tucked her in with hot water bottles and comforters. She was drawn to the crackling fire in the fireplace and we kept it stoked day and night.

She told her Dad that her closet needed shelves, immediately. So John bought a closet organizer system and, with Susie propped up in bed and directing his every move, he installed it.

A Texas friend called me, "I was so afraid she was going to die down here and you wouldn't be with her," she said. It was another reminder of the concern and caring people felt for us - and of their pain. I tried to comfort her: "I've always known that would not happen." We received a letter from Ann Parks, one of Susie's favorite nurses. She wrote, "All of us who took care of Susan were truly impressed with her. Our hopes and prayers are that she will continue to grow and flourish like the beautiful flower she is."

⊷━◉ ◎━⊶

As we settled into our new routine, I received information from Patrick McGrady and his organization, "CanHelp," and learned of Dr. Glen Warner, a leading holistic oncologist and immunologist whose office was in Seattle. I made an appointment for the first week in February, and we were introduced to a grandfatherly man who exuded kindness and respect.

He examined Susie and then stepped back and said, "You're late getting here."

"I'm here now," she said, looking into his eyes.

He asked to talk to me and led me to another room. He gently asked me, "Is she prepared to die?" I fell apart, crying. "She's prepared to live. She's a fighter. We've come for help, not to quit."

He told me she was very sick; her body had been damaged by the cancer and chemo. I knew that, but asked him to fight for her and not underestimate her.

Dr. Warner went back into Susie's room and told her he was going to help her fight. He changed her diet: no meat, except organic, for the hormones and toxins were too much for her liver and system; no sugar, for it stimulated cancer cell growth; no peanut butter, but she could have almond butter. Everything should be organic, to avoid hormones and pesticides. She would begin a massive vitamin regime. He started her on IVs full of nutrients to support and stimulate her immune system. He gave her shots to help balance her system. He told her that the body was a whole system, and that attacking cancer with chemo often damaged the whole. He had her listen to meditations on healing while her IV was administered.

Susie immediately felt comfortable on Dr. Warner's program, and she looked and felt better, too. She looked at me, while receiving her IV, with just the two of us in the room, and said, "Mom, he is the first person who has talked sense in two years."

Yes, I agreed, and I was wildly hopeful the tide could be turned, otherwise why had I been given the message: "You can heal. It's of the mind?"

⊷━◉ ◎━⊶

Healing is not a matter of mechanism; it is a work of spirit and we need to study those conditions that further that work. We need to remember that at the very heart of spirit is mystery. And the problem with the mind is that the mind cannot tolerate mystery.
Rachel Naomi Remen, Noetic Sciences

During this time, I sought out Lorie, an intuitive healer who was also a nurse. John, Susie and I went to the first appointment, where we talked awhile before Lorie began working with Susie in another room.

I was feeling ungrounded and hurting. I knew Lorie sensed my emotions, but Susie thankfully ignored them. Lorie quietly looked at me, and before she left the room put on a music tape. The music, new to me, reached out to me as I lay my head against the arm of the couch, exhausted. "Om Namah Shivaya" was the title. I felt myself instantly in a desert space filled with spirit and mystery. I will always associate this music with Lorie.

When the two eventually emerged from the bedroom, Susie looked very peaceful.

"While Lorie was working on me," she said on the way home, "I felt no pain for the first time in a long time." Lorie had not touched her, just sat in a chair by the bed. "It felt as if there was movement within me," Susie said. "There was sensation, but no pain, as if my body was trying to heal itself."

Lorie talked to us about what she had "seen" going on within Susie, and it was more detailed than anything we had had the energy or words to share with her. Susie had two more sessions with Lorie, and each time she experienced the lifting of physical pain and a sense of healing within her abdomen. Indeed, her color and her energy level were also better after these sessions. Still, my intuition told me, that while Lorie felt she could offer comfort, Susie would not remain with her body.

⇢⊱══◉═══⊰⇠

Susie was feeling better, but her abdomen continued to swell, and blood vessels stood out on her back, trying to relieve the internal load on her vascular system. The reality was dawning that our enormous hopes were not to be. Susie's cancer was too far advanced, and her body too damaged to turn the tide. But, we will be forever grateful she was under Dr. Warner's care the last six weeks of her life.

⇢⊱══◉═══⊰⇠

Three times a week, we gathered up Susie's pillows and headed down to Dr. Warner's office. Sometimes, Susie would get the "Mt. Rainier Room" for her treatment. "Ah…very special," she would declare. And always an unrushed meeting with Dr. Warner, who started calling her "Miss Texas."

Some people just seem to appear at the right time. John's Uncle Franklin unexpectedly came to town and spent a few days with us. She adored this uncle, and they held hands, as he kidded her, with a twinkle in his eye, just as he had when she was six years old. Seven years earlier, towards the end of my mother-in-law's sixteen year battle with cancer, Franklin drove from Wisconsin to St. Louis to surprise his sister.

In town to visit her, we heard footsteps, and the door burst open as he suddenly filled the room. He gave Mom a big hug, while she laughed up at him, her day transformed by his visit.

-->====()====<--

We had another snowfall in March, beginning on the day that Aunt Betsy came to visit. I tried to hurry Susie through the grocery store as the snow fell faster and heavier. She and Betsy thought it was great fun when the car ended up halfway in the street and halfway in our driveway, then slowly slid down to rest against our mailbox. I was worried about Susie falling, but she was having a great time.

-->====()====<--

About two or three weeks before Susie left, a young man called and asked if she would like to go to a movie. As she was having a good day, she accepted his invitation and carefully dressed. They went to a theater, where they had to wait in line to buy their tickets.

Susie, looking very pregnant because of her swollen abdomen, stuck her hands into her pockets, pulled her blouse close to her body and pushed her belly out a bit more. She loudly said, with much angst in her voice, "When are we going to talk about getting married? Look at me, our baby is coming! Why don't you want to get married? We have to talk about it. I don't know what to do. What is going to happen to our baby?"

Susie came home, exhausted but giggling. "The line of people stopped talking and just stared at us," she said. She hadn't planned on doing it. "It just came, Mom."

Susie could also do a great imitation of the Whiner, a wonderfully funny character on Saturday Night Live. We cracked up whenever she would start "whining" about something. "But Dad.... I don't waannt to."

Months later, this young man took me to lunch, and smiling, told me the movie story, saying he was so embarrassed he could have sunk into the pavement.

I patted him and exclaimed, "You've been Susied."

-->====()====<--

The first part of March, my women's group met at our house and Susie joined us. She told one member she had a dream of a room full of clocks all stopped at the same hour. The group was supportive and loving, and Susie enjoyed our peaceful meditation.

One week before she passed, early in the morning, I was jarred awake with the knowing that she had decided to leave. I "heard" her decision, and I received it.

I lifted myself up in the bed, crying, "Oh God! No."

My heart was pounding and I could hardly breathe. I walked on wooden legs to Susie's room, sending her my own thoughts: "Susie, I heard you, I heard you." She was sleeping peacefully. I marveled how in looking at my grown daughter, I could still see my baby daughter. I was bewildered that her presence could cease to be.

What I remember most about myself during Susie's last week was my anger. Sometimes I felt in a rage that she was leaving, and if my will could have torn down a mountain, it would have been leveled. In my mind, I could explode huge granite boulders.

I never ceased to believe in healing, in miracles; I prayed and asked God and the Universe for just that. Susie had been losing weight, most obviously in her face and upper body, but still she could attract glances from young men wherever she went.

My incredible daughter. I felt helpless and was frantic to keep her - to halt this tide that wanted to wash us somewhere else. I felt frustrated that my loving and mothering seemed to have so little impact.

Thus shall ye think of all this fleeting world: a star at dawn, a bubble in a stream; a flash of lightening in a summer cloud, a flickering lamp, a phantom, and a dream.

Buddha from the Lotus Sutra

CHAPTER 9

NO MORE

To the world you may be one person, but to one person you may be the world.
Rabbi Joseph Heller

The thing I remember most about Susie's last week "in her body," was her loving luminescence and that she didn't respond in the old ways to teasing or externals; she had transcended in some way. She had arrived at a wisdom and peace that most of us can only imagine - the "mindfulness" written about in Eastern religious teachings. Susie's gaze, the way she held things, sat in the car, touched our cat or her things, her response to others – all lovingly, and all very much in the moment.

That weekend Susie spent a lot of time on the couch leaning against her Dad, his arms wrapped around her. She would sometimes tease about giving him white hair, which was rather truthful. She called us her "parentals" and told us how wonderful we were. We wrote each other notes everyday, and I left one every night on her bedside table.

⊷══◉◉══⊷

Late one night I tiptoed in to check on Susie. I found her awake and in a lot of pain, her swollen abdomen radiating heat. She said, "Mom, help me."

"It's going to be all right," I said. I ran downstairs, grabbed several small icepacks out of the freezer, and ran back. I lay a towel over her abdomen and layered the cold packs on top. I had her swallow some of her liquid morphine. I gathered her into my arms and held her as she quietly cried. She seemed so very young as I cradled her.

Our friend, Virginia, who was spending the night, came into the room for a few minutes. Susie asked if she was going to "make it" and Virginia and I both replied, "Yes, you are."

I don't know if I should have answered yes or no to her question; I only know I believed she could heal. Susie wrote me notes thanking me for always believing that, for telling her she could and would heal. It was not a lie - I knew in my soul that healing was possible.

As I lay with Susie, held her, I told her everything was going to be all right. I told her how wonderful she was, and what a gift she was in my life and in the lives of so many others. I also told her nobody could drive me to the wall like she could. She smiled.

I told her that I believed with all my being in a Universe that was loving and powerful, and that she was a magnificent "prize." That there was so much more going on than we could see or understand. I held her, giving her my love and energy, and I visualized her surrounded with love and light. I told her everything was going to be all right. I rotated the ice packs that night, and her abdomen slowly cooled. She slept.

⤞⟫⟢⟢⟨⟨⤝

Dr. Bernie Siegel wrote, "*When doctors and patients understand the healing power of love, we will begin to add another dimension to medicine. Then we will be on our way to the glorious revelation predicted by Teilhard de Chardin in these famous words: Someday, after we have mastered the winds, the waves, the tides and gravity, we shall harness for God the energies of love. Then for the second time in the history of the world, man will have discovered Fire.*"

⤞⟫⟢⟢⟨⟨⤝

Susie attended a seminar by Dr. Siegel at Unity Church in Seattle. We drove to the seminar with pillows and a small ice chest full of Susie's food, drinks and medicine. She spent the day with the people in the seminar, and did two color drawings of herself and her illness. Toward the end of the seminar, she told Dr. Siegel, "I think I'm dying." I watched as he gently held her and they talked. John and I drove home with our golden daughter propped in the back seat, surrounded by a cloud of pillows.

⤞⟫⟢⟢⟨⟨⤝

She had an appointment the next day with Dr. Warner to have her IV "cocktail," as she called it. This time I sat above her head and held her hand while the IV dripped, and again I received her thoughts, her message.

Wordlessly, she said, "No More." I heard her distinctly, and I marveled at the clarity of our communication.

"I heard you," I answered her with my thoughts. "I understand, Susie. It's all right. It's all right."

In my heart, I understood. She had fought a courageous and noble battle. Her body had been through enough. "No more." I sat there and held her hand as my body ached and the tears rolled down my face.

We went to the reception room where several other patients were waiting. Susie sat in one of the chairs, surrounded by pillows, while I stood at the front desk. Helen Warner came out to talk to us and said, "Susie, your Mom is so pretty."

I turned around to smile my appreciation to Helen and found Susie looking at me. I felt her eyes were reaching into my soul.

With such presence and love, she quietly said, "My Mother is as beautiful inside as she is outside."

I was speechless and fought back the tears. The gifts I received from my daughter felt monumental.

~◆~

We didn't have much company drop by until what was to be her last week, and, in retrospect, I'm amazed at the people Susie drew to her - I like to think they answered her "summons."

My friend, Bonnie, called to arrange a visit with Susie and caught me at an overwhelming time: I needed to do some errands but did not want to leave Susie alone. She came and they had a great visit. I stopped by the house with my friend Diana to check on them and Susie was sitting up on the couch, surrounded by pillows, with a blanket tucked around her, looking fragile, poised, and beautiful. The air felt lively and loving around their conversation and laughter.

Another friend dropped by for a visit and sat on the couch across from Susie. She was going through a difficult and emotional time of change and she talked to Susie about it while Susie listened and absorbed the words like a wise and compassionate guru. "You are having a hard time with this. What are you going to do about it?"

To a woman twice her age, Susie was the acknowledged elder. As they talked more, their words blended to a soft rhythm in my mind. These were timeless moments that I witnessed and absorbed. I marveled at Susie and also at the possibilities and potential we each hold within ourselves. Are we more powerful than we know?

~◆~

On Friday afternoon Susie and I went out for a few errands. At the grocery store we slowly moved down the aisles with Susie leaning on the cart. Her face looked thin, and her abdomen swelled out to make her look quite pregnant. As always, she had makeup on, her hair was done, and she carried herself with dignity. I took her to the mall by our house to get some maternity hose and I will never forget her graceful, determined steps. Veering away from me, she stopped a pregnant woman to ask her where she bought her hose.

The two young women talked and laughed, the one never suspecting the other's reality. She smiled at an old couple sitting on a bench, and they returned her smile. She spoke to a small, crying child and slowly transformed his tears into a smile. I was an observer as my daughter touched these people's lives.

Driving home, I took a route that gave her a view of the city. It was dark and Seattle and Bellevue sparkled like many jewels. I pulled over and Susie just stared at the sight, absorbing it. She said, "Look, Mom. It's beautiful."

⸕⸙⸕

That night, our friends, Pat and Donna, came for dinner, and unexpectedly our friend, John, knocked on the door and we urged him to stay as well. Susie joined us at the table but did not eat. I was conscious of her every movement and expression as she made shapes with two small "pink panthers" on the table and talked with us.

Afterwards, we went to the den and sat on the couches while Susie lay on the floor in front of the fire, pillows around her. The warm fire filled the room with its smell and sounds. She seemed very tranquil, and would smile and sometimes join in our talk. Seated behind her, tears ran down my face in this bittersweet moment in time. I knew somehow that this moment belonged to Susie and thought, "Oh my daughter, you've danced this earthly dance so well." As the evening drew to a close, Susie reached up and gave each person a hug goodbye.

John and I cleaned up the kitchen and turned out the lights. Susie, lying in front of the fire, was lit with dancing shadows.

"It's time for bed, Daughter," I said.

I helped her upstairs and into nightclothes, tucked her into bed, and her Dad came in to kiss her goodnight.

⸕⸙⸕

Saturday morning Susie felt awful. I sat on the floor and held her in my lap and she turned toward me and asked, "Mom, is everything going to be all right?"

I said, "Yes Honey, it is."

She asked, "Do you promise?"

And I said, "Yes, I promise you. I promise it's going to be all right."

That was the last real verbal communication we had. Susie was in the process of leaving, and her body was shutting down. She tried to talk to her Dad but the words would not come. It frustrated her so. She kept saying, "Dad... Dad," and then she would say, "I'm... dammit!"

John picked her up and put her on the bed, and she began rocking motions.

When we called Dr. Warner, he said, "Her brain is probably swelling and she needs medication to reduce the swelling." He said he would send an ambulance and meet us at the hospital.

John answered, "No, she would hate that. We'll bring her." He carefully carried her down the stairs. While he drove we talked to her, and I held her in the back seat.

At the hospital, Dr. Warner said the medicines to reduce the brain swelling needed time, and that it might be "the beginning of the end." Susie was calm and resting now. Her eyes were staring at an unseen spot above her bed. Dr. Warner said she was in a coma.

After several hours, I told John to go home to get some rest and he left about 11 p.m. I sat near Susie, talking to her and telling her how much we all loved her. When it became more difficult for her to breathe, I called John. He arrived about 2 a.m.

The two of us stood by Susie's bed, holding her hands. She was unresponsive.

"Dad and Mom are here, Susie," I said. "We're here with you. We love you, Daughter."

Susie's eyes, which for hours had been unfocused and staring at the ceiling, slowly moved down and clearly focused on us.

"Susie, we love you, Darling. We're here, Honey."

Her Dad kept talking to her. "You're going to be all right, Susie. Mom and I are here."

Susie's eyes looked at us, and we knew she was seeing us clearly.

I felt myself holding my breath with the wonder of this moment, the absolute knowing that she was speaking to us with her eyes. She looked at me - into my eyes for several long seconds - then her eyes moved to her Dad's and she held the focus for another long instant. Those beloved, expressive eyes that could speak volumes were holding us, communicating.

Then her heart stopped beating. Her breathing simply ceased into stillness.

PART TWO

CHAPTER 10

A CHILD OF THE UNIVERSE

Silence.

I heard myself say, "Oh, Susie, please don't leave me."

The young nurse said, "I'm sorry, but she's gone."

I replied, "We know. Please leave us." She closed the door and left us alone.

I knew then that Susie had refused to leave until her Dad had returned, until she could say goodbye to both of us - until once more we had witnessed her powerful intention and spirit. I knew this was a gift from her, another example of her determination, her enormous will, and her love.

Another knowing: her spirit surrounded us still, though it was no longer in her body or even where my arms could reach. The room held her presence; I sensed her and felt her. John and I both knew that we must talk to her, must support this leaving, must express our gratitude and love.

"Susie, we thank you for being in our lives, for being our daughter," I told her. "We love you and thank you. You did it so well, Susie, you did it so very well."

We stood, looking at her still body and feeling her beautiful spirit.

John spoke, "It's all right to leave, Susie. We will be all right, and you will, too. We want you to go where you need to go. Our love will always be with you."

I lay down on the bed and wrapped my arms around her, and saw how beautiful she was. I stroked her face and traced a vein on her right cheek and jaw, and admired again the way her hair fell back from her forehead, her small perfect ears, her neck. I touched my daughter I had given birth to, and had watched grow and evolve into a young woman. Her Dad and I held and stroked her hands, her beautiful hands. We stayed with her until we knew it was time to go.

->==()==<-

"How can I be walking outside under this beautiful sky full of stars?" I thought, looking up, not comprehending. We drove home.

John made coffee, and we sat on the floor of the den with two friends. It was five o'clock in the morning. I said, "We never talked about this with Susie, what she would want done…" We knew Texas was home to Susie, so we must honor that, but the Northwest was home, too. Would Susie have wanted cremation or burial?

Then I heard Susie tell me, "Mom, I don't want any part of that body." At that instant, I knew that she wanted cremation of her "earth body," the body that had held so much pain and become so distended with disease; she did not want it. I spoke this aloud and our friend replied, "Then that's what you must do."

Around seven, the doorbell rang and our friend Donna stood at the door. I looked at her in my daze, saying, "Susie's gone." I asked, "How did you know?" There was no one who could have told her.

"I just knew," Donna said. She had brought Susie so much joy, laughter and loving, and thoughtful gifts during the last year. Somehow she knew.

Later, when the house was full of people, my hearing and sight seemed to be operating on a different frequency. Sounds came from a distance, and my mind recorded flashes of visual impressions: John sitting on the floor in front of the stereo, the house full of music and emotion as he chose what to play at the service. The voice of Toni Childs filling the house, melting my heart with her song, "Walk With The Angels."

I will forever hear and feel the words, "Walk, walk and talk, like angels talk…" Joe Crocker singing, "You Are So Beautiful To Me."

John took care of me. He led me to the table to eat, guided me upstairs and put me to bed, carefully arranging the covers. So strongly feeling Susie's presence and love, John and I listened for her communications to guide us in what to do. Later, looking for him through the house, I found him in the garage, his head bent in writing words he would later say at the service:

My special, special Susie,
I miss you deeply, for you changed my life and taught me so much.
Your smile inspired me and your spirit moved me.
How your light kept shining throughout your ordeal is an inspiration
that I will never, never forget.
You were our sunshine and brought us joy beyond words.
You touched people wherever you went with your energy.
I loved the way you met life head-on and lived each day fully.
For you, life was meant to be enjoyed, not endured.
You had a unique ability to move those around you to enjoy life with you.
I can't imagine a day without you in my thoughts, and I will hold you in my soul forever.
You are truly a child of the universe.
I love you.

Next day, John said, "I want to see her one more time."

With Virginia and Reine, we drove to the funeral home and walked inside where we were led to a small, softly lit room. My eyes and heart were hungry to see her.

We entered the room where Susie lay. Her body looked beautiful with that beloved profile, her golden hair, her perfect hands. But there was nothing left of her spirit. I marveled that I could not feel her presence or her spirit in this room. I remember standing still and saying, "There's nothing of Susie here. She's not here."

John and I approached and touched her hair, her face, her hands; the body she had left behind. But her essence, her spirit, was gone.

Strange that I felt Susie's presence so completely in our home, but not here. At home, I almost felt that her presence was so full and strong that I was bumping into her.

I later recalled the times we had called each other, and she knew my thoughts at the time and I hers; the moments when she had been troubled and I would know, as if an invisible current connected us. I experienced the same invisible current in these moments after she left when I "heard" her wishes for her body and sensed so strongly her support for us, and now, sensing so fully, her love and compassion.

We could still "hear" her thoughts to us clearly. This freedom of communication had not changed. Susie and I had always "felt" each other, and often responded whether we were rooms, or states, apart. The impact of really knowing this was very powerful for both John and me.

Reine told me that the moment spoke clearly to her of the power of the soul, how the soul or spirit is the engine of the body, and how powerful Susie's spirit is.

Loved Ones, she is not gone — she is the wind, the flowers, the trees, the mountains and the sky. She is the beloved Child of God, of you and John. She is and always will be a joy to all whose lives she has touched. Our tears are for you and John, not for our Susie, whose valiant spirit is now soaring above all the pain and is once more free to be with God. Nothing can take away the love we all have for her. The poor diseased body is now at rest — but the spirit of Susie is free and joyful with our Lord God."

Love, Grandmother Pat Kirby.

John and I stepped to the front of the hushed chapel at the memorial service, each of us taking a tall, lighted candle.

We walked down the aisle, lighting the candles held by the friends who surrounded us. Flame was slowly passed from candle to candle down each row, until the room took on a golden glow that danced and moved. It was beautiful to see so many rows and rows of candlelight. I knew Susie felt this love and beauty. Her presence was radiating in the flames.

Later, I would hear from people who had seen or felt my daughter during her memorial service.

What is seen passes away…. What is unseen is eternal.

So began the service by Laura Cameron Frazier, pastor and friend. It was a beautiful service, and I thought it would be appropriate to print in full here:

When someone twenty-two years old goes forth out of this life, we're inclined to say, 'What a tragedy.' A person so full of promise, so young in years, just on the verge of entering into her life…. What a tragedy when a person of this age and promise should be cut down.

Is it not the case this is the way we look at it and think about it? And I do not for a moment deny the reality of those feelings. It is one side of the picture. There is another side to it, and I would bring that side to you.

This afternoon I was walking in the hills close to my home, thinking about Susie, thinking about all of you, and I happened to look up. There is a path that leads through the trees and there are mountains about, and I looked just over on my left and I saw a cloud captured in the indentation of the hills there. It was quite beautiful to look at. As I looked about, I saw others.

I couldn't help but think, human life is lived as though it were under a cloud cover. We do not see the total picture. We see a limited part of it. And what seems tragic to us may not be tragic at all.

There is in the design of the soul a purpose. And when we come into this life, we come with this purpose. We may not always know this, but we decide what it is we will do here. We decide on our own experience. It is not perhaps widely known, but an individual must give permission before he goes forth. Our lives are more in our own hands than we might imagine.

So I am going to draw another scenario for you than the one I have just depicted. The scenario perhaps for Susie's soul. Here we have, without question, a beautiful soul, a beautiful spirit. Why did she come in for such a brief life span, then go forth? The human mentality says she contracted a fatal disease and she died. But what is the situation in actual fact?

I would suggest to you what I understand it to be, that before she came into this life she made her plan, because for a short lifetime, I see evidence of someone very intense, who lived life to the fullest, as if it were part of her plan. There was an intense living of life to its fullest. Now the universe is a large place and is full of many things. 'In my Father's house are many mansions.'

This soul had another destiny, another appointment to keep, a date in time. This life needed to be brief, and thus it was lived very intensely and fully. When she came into this life, she contracted with John and Mollie to be her parents, and to give to her the support she needed, the help and assistance she needed.

What is it she needed? What did this soul need? It is very true, yes, that she gave everywhere she went and that she was a light everywhere she was. What did she need? She needed to complete this experience before going on to another, and the experience she sought was to be fully, wholly, vibrantly aware of who she was, no matter what was going on in the body, in the immediate material life.

It was to live a life triumphantly whole in the spirit and not be stricken down by disease. This was something she already knew, otherwise she could not have led this experience through in this way, but she seemed to have needed to, shall we say, "set it," to know that she knew it, to live it through. That would leave no doubt of the strength she had. For this, she needed parents who loved and supported her through this experience, and this she had.

I am portraying for you a life from the perspective of the soul. A perspective that is under the cloud cover. We don't see it. Some learn to see this perspective. I suggest to you that this soul saw more of this perspective than any of us do. And that she did indeed fulfill her purpose in life. That she came into it and did exactly what she set out to do. That she left fulfilled and completed.

So you, John, and you, Mollie, did your work well. You fulfilled promises made. This is my understanding, of this spirit to whom you gave passage and shelter and loving care and protection and support. It is a job well done. Do not think therefore that because this life was brief it was unfinished. It was magnificent, just as it was.

And it is the case, John, just as you said, that you never have to live a day without Susan, because she is, she IS absolutely a part of this universe. She never will cease to be, not only a part of it, but part of you. Nothing can ever take her from you and nothing can ever take you from her. And that is the case for you, Mollie. There is no separation in actual fact in this universe.

Then Laura led a prayer for Susie's ongoing life and for her healing from her experiences while she was here. She ended the prayer with, "This soul is light, divine light. Thank you, Susan, for all you are."

The candle flames danced with light and life, confirming Susie's radiant participation in this gathering. I didn't see her, but I felt her joy.

After the Seattle memorial service, John and I left for Texas. In a canvas bag, clutched under my arm, I carried the urn. John and I knew that part of Susie belonged in a special place in the Texas hill country. We knew, too, that part belonged in a beautiful stream high in the Washington mountains she loved to hike.

Texas Christian University in Fort Worth offered their campus chapel for the service. We knew the service would a celebration of her spirit and life. We told Susie's friends that this was theirs, too, and we trusted they would create what they felt. I knew there must be light, and wanted individual candles for people to hold. To us,

Susie was light.

We stayed at the Williams' house, our familiar haven in Colleyville. The chapel at T.C.U. was filled with friends. Pastor John Butler led the service. Her friends had created a program, "Memorial Service of Thanksgiving for the Life of Susan Elizabeth Swope," and in it had written:

Susie believed in palm reading, existentialism and herself.

She doubted Lee Harvey Oswald acted alone, that there really is a devil and that God made cancer.

Susie fought for independence, understanding and life.....she sought fellowship, peace of mind, and 'a reason for things not understood.'

Susie cherished Monet, poetry and friendship.

She loved spaghetti with white Zinfandel, a walk in the park on a beautiful day, and most cats.

Susie hated frowns, a messy room, and organ music.

She abhorred typing Comp Two Papers, uncoordinated outfits on her friends, and the hospital.

Yet Susie relished typing papers for friends, lending her clothes, and coming home.

She's home now, at last. May we bless others as she blessed us.

May we celebrate the life that was, but more importantly,

the spirit that will always be.

We will miss you, Susie.

Our friend Eddie flew into town to play her flute at the service. Her music was incredibly beautiful, and I felt blessed she was there. Susie's friends were so loving as they rose and spoke from their hearts, and played their special music.

·▶═◉═◀·

Several years later, Kathy Kitchens Lyda shared with me her memories of this day. She called it, "A Sparrow's Song" and her words still touch John and I deeply.

St. Patrick's Day. A day for celebration, wishes of luck and green beer, a day to say good-bye. As I approached the college chapel I noticed how beautiful the campus was in spring. Trees budding with life, flowers celebrating with dashes of brilliant color and green, green St. Patrick's Day grass. The breeze was warm and gentle.

I had the driving need to be at the chapel before anyone else. When I arrived I wondered why. No flowers, no people, just the unique silence a place of worship holds when not filled with believers. Sunlight streamed through the windows and onto the pews, as if preparing a palette of light for those soon to be seated. I slowly walked down the main aisle, needing and yet dreading the upcoming day's events.

I ascended the stairs and busied myself with the necessities of the afternoon service. I had worked hard to make sure it was perfect from my end. Ministers apprised, music sifted through, friends notified.

Poem written, rewritten, torn up, and written again. To be read…by me…in front of all those people who loved her, too. In front of her parents, fellow classmates, former teachers, old friends, new friends, and some like me who were a little of both. What words could possibly mean anything?

I already knew what words didn't. The scream of the school newspaper headline, Student Succumbs to Cancer, still echoed in my thoughts. Written by someone who didn't even know her. At all. Someone who didn't see the fight, who didn't share in the healing. My face still flushed, thinking about the newspapers stacked neatly at first and then not so neatly by the end of the day by each classroom door. Succumbs. Succumbs. Before each midterm I took that day the word assaulted me. As I walked to and from class the papers seemed everywhere. Scattered in the halls, crumpled up and blowing in the wind outside, stuck underneath desks. Fellow students must have thought I was cracking underneath the pressure of mid-term stress as I frantically collected each folded, crumpled, stepped-on piece and crammed them into whatever receptacle was nearby. Succumbed indeed.…

I fervently prayed for strength to get through the next hour and a half without (that word again) succumbing to the overwhelming grief that had enveloped my life since hers ended here. I looked at my poem. Words so inadequate for a life so wonderful, a fight so valiant and a comrade so dear. Would she understand? Would those who loved her? Would I be belittling a Spirit so strong with words so seemingly weak? I shoved the poem in my pocket as the minister and her parents walked in, and welcomed them. Enough reflections for now.

I was amazed how many people fit into the tiny chapel as I peered over the podium. The music had been beautiful, the minister's words consoling, and now there was me…at the podium…with a feeble declaration of her life's impact. As I began to read, my voice faltered.

I paused to steady myself and peered into the sea of people who now looked to me for… for what? I just didn't know. While gazing out into the crowd, my eyes locked with an old friend sitting in the middle of a pew crammed full with the many young faces present. Something drew me past his tears and out the doors of the chapel, which were opened on the warm spring day.

A sparrow had perched herself on the chapel's stair landing and at that moment decided to sing to her heart's content. Her chirps were loud and clear, and captured the essence of what my poem struggled to convey. Although her euphony lasted only a few seconds, it was long enough to celebrate the life of a friend.

In those few seconds she shared a message I carry with me to this day. The service was not about my words, her chirps, or biblical verse. It was about the grandeur of grief. A sadness so deep over the loss of a person so treasured. New valuation, acceptance and release of the fight she had fought. Overwhelming love for the person that was and the Spirit that is. Words would never do her justice. Only a collective consciousness drawn from the depths of the souls who knew her.

As I finished reading my poem, I knew I had contributed my piece. A single note in a symphony of retrospection, emancipation, and celebration. But a note nevertheless.

⋘⋙

The next morning John and I left for the hill country, between Austin and San Antonio, knowing and trusting we would be led to the perfect place. John, without hesitation, drove off the paved roads until he stopped at a place we both knew, without words, was right. The horizon was gentle with layers of blue hills and we could see for miles, as a warm breeze touched and embraced us. We talked to Susie as we scattered her ashes, telling her we knew a part of her would always be here, surrounded by country she loved. Afterwards, we drove to San Antonio and spent time with my dad and my stepmother, Pat. Kandi's mother, Mary Francis, brought me a soft throw blanket, "to wrap around you when you need comfort."

⋘⋙

In the aftermath of Susie's leaving, we were comforted by the love and memories friends shared with us. They reminded us vividly of Susie's spirit and the gifts she had given people. A note from Susie's beloved nurse, Pat: *"I have known many patients since I began working in hospitals in 1969, but never have I been as touched as I was by Susie. The last thing she wanted was for anyone to feel sorry for her. She loved her family and her friends, and knew they loved her. You should be proud of Susie, as I am sure you are always. She was a loving and giving person. I want to thank you for sharing her and a part of yourself with me."*

⋘⋙

John's cousin Glorian wrote: *"Susie was such a special person. Her own person. Even when I first met her as a little girl about six years old, she was already becoming her own person. Then when I saw her again as a teenager… what a joy! She was like a breath of fresh air. You, her parents, did a good job of helping her develop into that lovely person that we will always remember. She touched so many people's lives and was an inspiration to all. I feel so fortunate that I had the opportunity to know Susie. As her life was an inspiration to those around her, so will the memories of her continue to inspire and brighten the lives of those who knew her."*

⋘⋙

I wrote, *Like a buoy at sea, I rock from side to side, sensing no safety from this force that clumsily carries me along. There is no escape from this time or place and all feels strange, even John's strength and love that touches me, holds me. He and I are weary, in need of rest and comfort - we have surrendered but cannot answer to what. I cannot even begin to comprehend my world. Silent and bewildered, I begin another day.*

CHAPTER 11

INTO THE SILENCE

I think that most of life I've been anesthetized, in a bit of a twilight sleep, where I could function and talk and do, and a lot of feelings were just totally buried. But life has a way of forcing the truth on you.
Carol Burnett

Every first time was hard. The first time I looked into Susie's bedroom and saw her pile of pillows, opened the refrigerator and saw her medicines, and looked toward her place in the family room.

Wanting to hear the phone ring, a door slam, her voice call. Silence.

The friends and relatives have all gone home and there is nothing to distract from the reality of change. Susie "left" March 12, Sunday, at 2:25 in the morning. I miss her so much it is a wordless ache. Oh my daughter, I want you in my life, your friendship and our long talks. I want to go to movies and shopping with you, bum around like we so often did. To hear your car in the driveway, your footsteps and your voice calling, "Hi Mom!" I love you to say that.

⋅→⋅━━◦◦━━⋅←⋅

My body and mind were not working in unison, as if each thought took longer to carry out my intention. Even using a fork and knife, I couldn't judge the results well. Awkward, thinking I was walking straight, I would veer off. Grief scattered my balance and coordination. Simply walking or driving a car felt strange. I would find myself bumping into furniture, or climbing stairs and having to concentrate on each step.

The day John went back to work was a bottomless day - I did not think I could survive the grief or being alone. I called a friend who listened and then uttered timeless wisdom: "Go sit and be with it. The only way to get to the other side is to go through it."

I sat in a ball on the couch and surrendered. I felt as if I were moving; that I had no center or foundation. I grieved until I was exhausted, until the storm was over and a calmness settled over me.

Sometime later I read "A Gradual Awakening". In his book, Stephen Levine wrote, *It seems ironic that despite our conditioning to elude pain, our real work may be to bring love to our pain. To allow it a new openness and acceptance that have not been encouraged in the past. Not to hold it or to push against it. But simply to let it be in self-awareness and compassion, rejecting no part of ourselves. Surrender is perfect participation in the circle. Letting go allows us to flow, to become the whole circle. To hold to any point is to lose our original nature because there is no place we begin and nowhere we end.*

I had to learn that there was nothing to grasp "here," and I could only keep opening myself - a sensation like falling. I had been ultimately forced to surrender my will in my daughter's transition, to support and release her to her path, while receiving affirmation that her life was more than her human body experience. A surrender that happened again and again, as my human instinct rebelled against letting go.

Susie was no longer here, but I could still give her support and love with her choices and destiny - and thank her for being in my life. Her words, "Mom, it takes courage to live," floated through my consciousness.

⸱⸱⸱⸱⸱⸱⸱⸱

A note in the mail: *Susie was such a special person to all who had the privilege to know her. While she chose to be here, she gave so much, and understood such a great deal about the beauty and complexity of this earth. I remember most of all her sensitivity, gentleness… and that magnificent smile. One day she spoke a great deal about trees — particularly a dying oak outside her bedroom window in Texas. She said that she would pretend to sit in its aching branches and soothe it, visualize all of her love going into its limbs, down through the scarred trunk to the very roots. After several days she noticed that the tree began to sprout green leaves and that the branches began to point upwards, toward the sun. She felt very happy, she said, that perhaps her love had helped heal the tree. And so her love and beauty always will.* All my love, Cindy.

⸱⸱⸱⸱⸱⸱⸱⸱

One day the phone rang. Stephen, an intuitive and special friend, called to ask if John would come see him. "Susie has a message for John."

Stephen told him, "Susie was struggling before she left to express to you her love and gratitude for all you did for her." That last afternoon, Susan had been struggling to talk to John, frustrated that her failing body wouldn't let her do so. "She wants you to know how very, very much she loves you, and that she will be with you. She wants you to know how very grateful she is that you were her Dad."

⸱⸱⸱⸱⸱⸱⸱⸱

On Easter Sunday, John and I attended the service at Laura's church. The previous two days, I had felt Susie so close, and had awoken each morning to a rare sense of happiness and peace. I was not grieving or hurting, but experiencing a deeply peaceful joy that lasted day and night. I refused to question too closely this "place" I was in, for I felt this absence of pain was fragile.

We greeted Laura, and as she looked intently at me, she slowly observed, "You are in a state of grace."

"Yes, that must be true," I said. I felt deep blessings and quiet joy. So this is what "grace" feels like, this word I have heard about all my life. I also knew that no word could begin to express this feeling that acknowledged my earthly presence, and was also totally connected to something divine.

This "state of grace" held me for five days. The words, "She's taken me with her" moved through me. I was at ease and profoundly aware that I was not hurting. It was a most wondrous experience that I prayed would continue, but I came crashing back to earth one day, and experienced afresh the raw grief of separation. I will never forget the miracle of that week.

On April 30th I was jolted awake. I heard Susie tell me, "Mom, I'm at Zynanite." I felt sleep pulling me back, and Susie's voice came again, insistent and strong, "Mom, write it down! I'm at Zynanite!" (This is what it sounded like.) I sat up in bed, reaching for pen and paper. Susie was insistent I know this name, and the joy of hearing her voice was like water to my thirsty heart.

Later, I sat on my bedroom floor and meditated. Breathing slowly, stilling myself, I sent my love and gratitude to Susie and asked, "Let me see you as you are now." I sat quietly with my eyes closed, yearning to see her physical body, and then received a vision: a beautiful ball of swirling energy, glowing with blue, gold and white light. I sat still, trying to absorb this unexpected gift. Later that day, I was cleaning and while vacuuming her room, saw something sparkle by her bed. I knelt down and picked up a marble, clear with blue, yellow and white swirls in it. This room had been cleaned before this day and there had been no marbles anywhere with Susie's things. My body tingled all over with "shivers" as I held this treasure in my hand, and filled with wonder and gratitude, thanked her.

A dream in May of 1989:
Susie had an illness. She and I were walking across a very long modern bridge, looking much like the I-90 floating expanse across Lake Washington, as seen from the

Seattle side. We encountered people along the way and everyone knew they were saying goodbye. Most of the communication was done without words.

Susie wanted to buy crystals: We bought a crystal that looked mossy on top, a large stick of tourmaline, blue crystals and big chunks of different stones. We also bought clear rounded crystals, about the size of a small egg, and a large one the size of her hand.

She silently communicated to me that she wanted her friends to have these after she left. She knew I would carry out her wishes. She put the crystals in a cloth bag and threw the bag into a river or lake that moved with the tide. Susie had a sense that she must get everything done before she left, and she wanted to leave gifts behind.

I asked her how I was to give these to her friends, and she said, "Pull the string, it is tied to the bag."

I was with her when she left her body, thanking her, loving her.

The sky felt powerful, windy, the clouds rolling through profound spaces. I experienced pain, but not overwhelming grief. Shortly after she left, I went to pull the string to retrieve the crystals. I pulled and pulled on the string and came up with an empty knot. I was dismayed; I hadn't expected this. I gathered some of the crystals, but couldn't find the special large one: it was missing.

I crept down to the water, under the wide bridge, to find it. I looked but couldn't find it, then I looked further and saw brilliant, sparkling crystals scattered around, the tide washing over and moving some of them. Many had their bases in the sand, their large clusters of points reaching upward. I saw the clear, smooth, quartz ones, and remembered these were to be given to her friends; she had chosen them especially. The crystals were so very beautiful. I could reach and pick some of them up.

It was a magnificent treasure place, under the bridge - a private world, but one others could find. I wanted to collect the crystals before the water carried them away. I gathered some, so beautiful and varied, in my hands. I couldn't reach many and I was afraid if I entered the water after them, I might be swept away.

I looked back at the tide and knew I could make it. I lunged towards some large rocks, squeezed through, out and down, until I reached the crystals; I knew I would be all right. The tide washed over me, moving me with its rhythm.

These were prized treasures, sparkling lights and colors against the gray water and sand. Crystals in hand, I backed myself towards the opening, feeling wet and exhilarated, with the earth beneath me. I had lost the large crystal and the bag, but found this place and these treasures by following the string Susie had left.

·›══◉◎══‹·

In the months that followed, I could not say the words "Susie died" to others or myself, because she had changed – but still IS. It was not that I was denying her body had died, but that her essence, her spirit, plainly was vitally alive.

While her body held her life force, it was her spirit and our communication that I had felt, although we were states apart - as I had felt, too, when her body was hurting or needing help. She had been, to her great relief, released from her body. Now, although I was desperate to see her physically, it was her spirit that filled our space and made her presence known.

How could I say, "Susie died," when I felt her so alive? How could I say I "lost" her, when she did not feel lost, but only changed? So I said, "Susie left, or transitioned," and I say it still. For there is no word in the English language that feels right to me. Yes, there is an ending, a death for the body, but we cannot deny the essence of our loved ones. We cannot deny their spirit.

⇥▭◉▭⇤

The void Susie has left is so intensely felt. The words come to me, "I don't know what to do with the missing. It's all over and through me. There is no part of me that is spared. There is no place to turn or go." I mourn yesterday, today and tomorrow.

We realize the part she played in our world - her passion and life force made our lives more complete. I know that we lived some of our lives through her and her spirit. As a child and young adult, she acted as I wish I could or would have. John and I both gloried in her spirit, intelligence, and focus.

I know she is happy, undiminished and powerful where she is, but I miss going through life with this "totally alive human being." I long to see her charge into a room and light it up with her passion for living.

From my late teenage years, my vision had always included my child. Somehow, I had to write a new script, take unwilling steps each day into a new life. I had learned to endure as a young person with my mother's illness and death, but I felt beaten now that my daughter, too, was gone.

Like spokes on a wheel, our individual energies had met at a center and created their own unique whole. John and I felt a wedge had been cut out of our being and we would have to learn a new way to live, but the future was unthinkable without her.

I found myself grieving her leaving and also grieving anew the child in me who had been abandoned, yearning for a mother's love and strength. When I was a teenager, my mother's illness and passing had molded and exhausted me — but this, there was nothing like this. No one had touched my heart as my child had. No one could have driven me to the surrender that my daughter had. No one could have driven me against the wall - except my daughter.

My self-confidence and esteem often felt in shreds. Shaken to the core, I knew there was wonder itself in that realization, and knew too, " There is so much more going on than I can know."

⇥▭◉▭⇤

All the human emotions would barrel through with awesome force - or simply and powerfully rise up unexpectedly and take my breath away. During the first months I would curl up on my bed and feel as though I were being tossed by huge waves. I had to surrender myself to this powerful current of grief that left me limp and exhausted. I couldn't fight my need to grieve; I could only give in to this storm and lose myself in the hugeness of it.

My body often hurt and I could be triggered by seeing one of Susie's favorite foods at the store and be wracked instantly by sobs. The tears dripped as I listened to music or drove the car in silence. I was a sensory mess, with everything - sound, smell, sight - reminding me of Susie. There wasn't anything in the world that did not trigger some memory, remind me of the missing, of the physical loss, of the forever change.

I would wake up in the morning with my eyes full of hot tears, not wanting to be in this world of missing. John would lean over and hold me as we both breathed in another day.

→→===◯===←←

A friend called, several weeks after Susie left, to tell me he had seen her at the memorial service in Seattle.

I caught my breath. "You saw her?"

He assured me he had. "Susie," he said, "was hovering above the large flower arrangement, looking beautiful and healthy with long golden hair cascading down her back. She had on a magnificent dress of golden discs or coins that glowed. She was simply there, joyous and receiving the love from all the people before her.

"Then she raised her arms out to her sides, and with her hands open, she radiated love back to all the people." He said she was very beautiful, extremely happy, and very aware and appreciative of what was being given to her. "Then, still radiant, her image faded and disappeared."

This call came on a day when I was feeling clumsy and heavy with grief, and it transformed my day. Again, I was being reminded that Susie was so much more than her earthly experience.

→→===◯===←←

The wise in heart,
mourn not for those that live, nor those that die.
Nor I, nor thou, nor
any one of these
ever was not, nor ever
will not be.
Forever and ever afterwards.
Ancient Hindu

CHAPTER 12

COMMUNICATION

Hardly a day passes that Susie's passion for living and her youthful wisdom are not vivid and bright in my thoughts and dreams. From little on, she was often the first one up in the morning, but if I did need to wake her, I cannot recall a single time she did not open her eyes with a huge smile and want a wake-up hug. She would begin at "speed," usually singing or humming a tune and anxious to get going. If we had special plans for the day or a trip to take she would be out in front ready to soak in the new experience.

John Swope

Two months after Susie's passing, I received a beautiful Mother's Day card from my stepson, Todd. He followed it with a call. "Mollie, how are you doing?" I felt his love and genuine caring. John gave me one "from" Susie, which was exactly the card she would have picked. Had she helped him as he stood in the card shop?

A dream: *I am standing on an old stone bridge, with Susie below on a town square. She is ill and needs help. I run, my breath jagged; I run with leaden legs, to the stairs. I am frantic inside, aching as I rush down the steps. I reach her and wrap my arms around her as she leans into my body and my mother love.* I wake up so sad, crying deep sobs that make the tears run. I touch John and say, "Hold," and he gathers me into his arms, his touch and closeness offering comfort.

Susie loved to be held in her Dad's arms. It is so healing to be held and touched as the warmth seeps deep inside and one feels safe and loved. Could Susie ever feel safe, confronting what she did?

Sometimes I feel a panic and need a safe friend to "hold me." We all have these people in our lives. They are few, and each an enormous gift. I pick up the phone and call my friend, and she feels my pain and lets me cry and say the words, "This hurts too much," or "How I wish…"

My friend may murmur her caring, or share a memory, always offering healing words from her heart. No advice, just being with me. We may be silent for a moment, just conscious of our breathing, and I feel comforted.

Janice, on Mother's Day, sent me a bouquet of flowers with a card that read, "To a mother who taught us all courage."

Did I? It was my first Mother's Day without Susie and I felt overwhelmed and powerless. It was so hard letting her go. I thought, "If this is so, I am the most unwilling courageous person on earth."

→▸═◉═◆═◂←

John quietly announced this was the day to scatter the remainder of Susie's ashes in the mountains. Feeling wounded, I grieved all the way to Lake Katchiss, the place the three of us used to go for picnics and hiking. It lies away from the lake in a secluded wooded area overlooking a stream. The day was warm with sunshine, and the only sounds were the trees, the birds singing, and the rushing water. We ate lunch and lay on a blanket beneath the trees, soaking in the peace of the place.

John brought the urn and we walked to the stream. He said some beautiful words about Susie being free, about loving her. Then he scattered her ashes in the rushing stream. We watched as the water whirled and tumbled them away. I prayed for Susie to know how much she is loved; prayed to be able to let go of all limitations and to grow in wisdom. I kept trying to transform my sadness into joy and send it to her.

John teased that maybe "Stampede Pass" would have been a more appropriate place for Susie and we both smiled. As we sat together, I felt that Susie was near, sending us her love. I asked John if he felt Susie and he looked to where I, too, felt her presence, then looked at me and smiled. We shared this moment, each of us.

→▸═◉═◆═◂←

Mother's Day 1989.

There were many times our daughter "came" to be with us. I journaled: *Moving around the kitchen, fixing lunch, I can feel Susie's presence, though I can't see her. I reach for a cookie sheet and feel myself "bump" into her. I stop to look at the area where I sense her, and I talk to her, ask her questions, tell her I love and miss her. We communicate, without words, back and forth. She knows me to the depth of my being; I feel her humor, knowing and wisdom.*

I continue moving around the kitchen, and again feel a physical contact, as if she were bumping me, touching me, until I know without doubt that this IS. I talk to her, teasing her, "You know, you're still one fabulous daughter, and I love you." I walk down the stairs to open the garage door and say, "John, Susie's here."

He looks up and smiles. "Yes, I know, she's been out here with me." We share this joy of her presence and knowing, over and over again. Our intimacy and gratitude for these moments spills over and surrounds us, holding us as if we were holding her. Our reality and the gifts we receive shape our every experience.

One day, several months after her leaving, I felt that Susie was grieving and needing comfort, missing us. I felt it so strongly - I cried with the emotion as it swept through me. Susie, who gave so much love and support, needed it now. I told John what I felt, and we both sent her love and reassurance. She wasn't here in body, but she needed us at that moment, as a weary child needs comforting.

I felt this with all my being. John, intuitively, said he had been feeling Susie's sadness, too. I went inside to sit and send her my mother love, surrounding her with protective light, telling her everything was going to be all right. I reached out and "drew her" into my lap, rocked her and held her for a long time as I murmured, "You have 'your parentals' love and support forever, wherever you are. You, young lady, are stuck with us. Everything is going to be all right. Know this." I later meditated and received - that Susie and all spirits have an enormous "mother-force" to go to for comfort, that is incredibly nurturing, loving and healing.

A dream: *I am walking on the beach watching the ocean waves. I see a "wise one" sitting inside a small open cave, very close to the sea. She glows with the white light surrounding her. I approach and see the way to her is by a short path. I walk, and the path grows longer. I try one approach and can't reach her, so I enter a tunnel and walk forward. I can see the glow of the wise one, and I am determined to reach her. I walk, turning as the path turns, coming to a fork and seeing more paths. I know I will find my way.*

Several weeks before Susie left, I had taken her to my office. As I did some work she visited with my friends. Unbeknownst to me, she had lifted up a few "post it" notes and wrote, *I love you! Seattle and Bellevue, Washington State, USA, World and Universe! Look Out.*

It was many weeks after she left when I finally used the top notes and found her message. Overwhelmed and trembling, I left the office with another treasure from Susie.

At home, I found she had done the same thing with a notepad: *Dear Mom, Just a note to remind you how very much I love you! Have a Wonderful Day! Somebody loves you! Hey, That's me! Your Daughter, xxxx ooo.* I found this one weeks later and just sat, thanking her, unable to feel more than the moment.

People would sometimes comment on how well I was handling things, but no one saw the private world I lived in, when I lay my protection down. I no longer

regard people as I once did, for I realize we cannot begin to know someone by looking only with our eyes. I would buoy myself by saying, "I am my daughter's mother."
I would wrap Susie's jean jacket around my shoulders, looking down at her buttons,
especially the big one, "No Whining," that she often wore during her illness.

In the months and years to come after Susie's leaving, I always had to prepare
myself to be "out in the world." John and I might go to a dinner where children were
present, or talked about, or I would see a mother and daughter at the grocery store,
and my heart would ache and I wanted to crumble.

One day, I felt Susie forcefully communicate, *Mom, stay here now!*

I knew what she was telling me and I would repeat those words to myself, nar-
rowing my world, until nothing existed but this moment.

Right now, everything is all right. I know Susie is happy in her new realm. I will
not think about the past or the future. My "being in the moment" has helped me
through many hard times, and carried me again and again.

→➤▇◉▇◄←

As if the universe regarded me as a child needing to be reminded, there was
incident after incident that deflected my pain and made me appreciate anew the
powerful spirit that was my daughter - and that she IS. I felt I lived in two worlds:
the physical reality, with vivid memories of what her body had endured, and the
borderless love and compassion I knew was holding me.

I felt Susie around us constantly for the first four months after she left, deeply
appreciating our connection and communication. Then a day came when I did not
feel her and I knew she was no longer close.

My heart beating with anxiety, I sat and meditated and received the message that
she had gone far away to do some sort of study or work and that she would be back.
Again I received the knowing that in this lifetime she and I would always have this
strong bond of communication. I doubted, though, and worried that this couldn't
last. I was being challenged to trust life on a new level.

→➤▇◉▇◄←

About two weeks later, she was back and I felt her smile; I was "bumping into"
her again. A joyous bumping. I lit up and laughed. "Susie... you're back!" I was so
excited and thanked her, feeling from her that she had been in a sort of classroom,
learning. She was back, and I felt like celebrating.

I stood in my bedroom or kitchen and talked to my daughter who no longer had
a physical body. I felt her playfulness, her smile, and smiled and laughed with her,
living in my other knowing that she IS. Later, when I felt her presence gone again, I
did not panic as before. I rejoiced when I would feel her strong presence, as again

and again I experienced her leavings and comings. I was learning, in this uncertain place, to trust our bond.

->==) (==<-

John and I wanted to celebrate Susie's birthday. She would have been 23 years old on January 27, 1990. Our friends told us we were welcome to use their lake home on Whidbey Island. We gathered candles, a bottle of wine and headed north.

The ferry made its way across the winter water, and we drove through the forest-lined roads to the house. John built a fire that slowly sent warmth and light into the room. We set candles around as darkness fell, and the room grew more intimate with the crackling of the fire and candlelight.

John and I sat facing each other on either side of the fire. We talked to Susie and toasted her and thanked her for being our daughter. We told her we were celebrating this day she had been born. John told a couple of stories about things she had done, and we chuckled with our memories. We felt her presence and her love.

Then I felt her presence so strongly standing in front of us, facing the fire. She was smiling, laughing, and beaming at us, with her hands on her hips and her feet firmly positioned, as she used to stand. Loving on us. It was so real, I felt my breath catch as I tried vainly to see her, then I simply let myself feel her presence and give and receive love.

I said, "John, she's here."

He said, "Yes, I know." His head nodded toward the very same area. He said, "She's standing right there, with her hands on her hips, smiling at us."

I knew it was a gift the three of us were sharing, this moment of intimacy and love. John and I raised our glasses of wine to Susie's presence. "Susie, we toast you and tell you how very well you did it all. We love you and support you and miss you terribly. We are so grateful for this moment."

We felt her love, her presence, knowing she knew her parents loved her, and she loved us. We sat in quiet companionship with Susie. We were silent, yet the air seemed full of communication. The only sounds were from the crackling fire. Slowly time passed, and we knew we had celebrated this day well. Susie's powerful presence had left, and we sat until the fire turned into glowing embers. Grateful. Missing. Having. Knowing.

CHAPTER 13

A MOTHER'S GUILT

Forgiving ourselves is the wellspring of all true forgiveness. It is the deep work of the heart that allows us to grow toward the light instead of struggling constantly with the darkness.

Kent Nerburn

A mother's guilt is so hard to live with. It would wash through me and leave me heavy with "what ifs" and regrets. Knowing Susie's love and communicating with her did not keep me from these experiences. The enormity of her being gone, and the finality, seemed unbearable. I read somewhere, "Scratch a parent and you'll find guilt."

Reading the paper, or watching television, I would feel another parent's loss through accident or illness, and be filled with a deep compassion for the grief and pain that spans this world.

It seemed I bore the weight of all parents - of knowing we would do many things differently if we could do them over. Of wishing that our present wisdom could have benefited our loved ones. Of seeing the countless incidents and expressions on our children's faces, recorded in our minds and in our family albums.

Memories of leaving Susie at daycare when she was a toddler, of her arms reaching for me, her tears. Countless incidents flooded back, times when I could have been more patient, more loving, wiser. I recalled also many moments of laughter, of knowing I had made her life good - yet the regrets haunted me.

A mother wants to protect her child and keep her from harm. Why couldn't I? Why hadn't I known something was very wrong? Why couldn't we find someone who talked about immunology? Would it have helped her? Why couldn't anyone talk about a combination of treatments?

For two years I had known there were better ways than the traditional medical route, even though not one medical person talked about nutrition, the mind-body connection, the immune system, except, near the end, one special doctor. "The only one who talked sense," Susie would say, with a look of wisdom.

I fought this huge adversary - guilt. Although I still deal with these thoughts today, there has been much healing. There would come moments when I felt Susie being patient with me: "You'll get bored with beating yourself up, Mom, and stop." Yet, for a long time, no amount of remorse lessened my pain.

This, it was clear, wasn't what Susie was about, with her powerful loving spirit. It was my burden, my stuff, my learning...my door to open and walk through. With all the conflict we experience in this existence, we are taught again and again that what is real, what endures, is love - love without condition or boundaries. This word, love, that is so freely used; Susie patiently and insistently revealed its power to me.

In "Who Dies?" Stephen Levine wrote, *What are the feelings we so quickly label as love? For many what is called love is not lovely at all, but is a tangle of needs and desires, of momentary ecstasies and bewilderment. You cannot unconditionally love someone. You can only be unconditional love. It is not a dualistic emotion. It is a sense of oneness with all that is. The experience of love arises when we surrender our separateness into the universal. It is a feeling of unity. You don't love another, you are another. There is no fear because there is no separation.*

Healing with little prayers, deep breaths:

"I forgive myself for not being what I wished I had been."

Ultimately I realized that the biggest regrets in my life are the times when I did not act with love - towards others, or myself... towards life.

⟶⟫⟨⟶

A parent's guilt goes way deeper than words, than making sense. I have questioned what purpose this aspect of grief serves, and have come to see that it can lead to tremendous learning. It is not about the thinking process - you can think all day about what you did or did not do - but this reaches to an ancient level. As a mother, my instinct was to protect and keep my child safe. I felt an overwhelming sense of betrayal as my treasure, my child, was being threatened; I was losing the enormous gift that I had carried in my body. My "walls" had sheltered and nourished and protected her, yet I had now lost the ability to protect.

This was why my hands and womb ached: My ability to touch and nurture were denied me. This is where the mother guilt goes, deep inside to a pulsing instinct without the need for words or thoughts. At times the heart of my hands would ache and throb. I would cradle the hurt that sang through my body, being with these moments until I arrived at the other side. When we can reach through our pain to forgiveness, we touch something that feels holy.

⟶⟫⟨⟶

A friend wrote, *When you do cry, cry with a conscious thought that you are releasing and notice the thoughts that come up. Allow for past information to flow through you and most of all, forgive yourself. Love of self is the ultimate thing to work on.*

Only through your emotions can you encounter the force field of your own soul. That is the human passage in a word.

Gary Zukav, *The Seat of the Soul*

I let myself feel each emotion as it came to me, feeling at times, I would not survive the pain. I am here to find my way. I am here to know myself and experience love, without conditions or limits. I am here to live this life courageously and in awareness.

During meditations, I have felt Susie's arms swing wide as she tells me, "Mom, life is so much bigger than you know, and so are you."

Lord, why do I often feel so small and helpless? What knowledge and skills are there for me that I do not yet realize? I think if Susie could say something to the world, it would be, "Death does not exist, and choices do not make a tragedy." Life is eternal, and we "here" are asked to learn and live under limited perspectives and knowledge.

⌖

Sometimes before I go to sleep, I ask to visit my daughter. "Susie, I ask to be with you tonight, wherever you are." I often do not remember my dreams, but may awaken very peaceful, sometimes tired, as if I have been somewhere far away. There are times when I feel I have been with Susie, in some wonderful place, sometimes just she and I, but often with a joyful group of others. Although I may not remember dreams of that night, I feel a quiet happiness and do not experience the acute missing, the hard grief that day. I believe my spirit has spent time with her while my body was sleeping. I believe my asking is often answered. I believe the way I feel the next day is a telling of my night journeys.

⌖

Meditating in my bedroom one morning, I received from Susie: *Mom, I want you to love yourself as much as you love me.* With a jolt, I realized I knew well how to endure and to berate myself... but to love me?

Feeling Susie wanting me to do this, I still fought within about all the regrets in my life. Finally, taking some deep breaths, I quieted and visualized myself receiving the unending love I felt for my daughter, and cried with the utter sweetness of it. The love embraced my body, my hands, my heart, as if vibrating through me. I sat in silence, in awe, and gratitude.

When I turned that beautiful focus of love on myself, great healing occurred. Being open to my shadows and my pain did not destroy me. Accepting and giving love, I got to the other side, another place in my passage.

⟶▸══◉══◀⟵

Susie, last night I was lying in bed and felt you kneeling down, like you used to do in high school, whispering to me about your evening's adventures. So often, you would come in and touch my hand, "Mom, are you awake?" And I would turn to you, our faces close together, and you would tell me about an adventure with your friends, the ball game, a happiness or heartache, and I would stroke your hair, your cheek, loving this time together. All the times we giggled and whispered and Dad didn't wake up. Then you would scurry off to bed, and I would hear you, doors closing and opening. Knowing you were home safe.

CHAPTER 14

A HEALING PLACE

*The real healing of grief can't take place until we make
the journey from the mind to the heart.*
John E. Welshons

Susie loved the holidays and celebrations and the thought of our first Christmas without her was overwhelming. John arranged for us to go to England for he knew it was impossible for us to celebrate the holidays as before. Aching inside we left for England, relieved to be leaving the familiar behind. We stayed at his company's flat in Windsor for a few days, then spent the rest of the time driving the south of England, finding lodging when night fell. We explored Wells, Bath, Salisbury, Lyme Regis, and Canterbury, and just let our days happen. John drove us into London and we spent hours walking through Hyde Park, St. James Park, Westminster Cathedral, Harrods and the British Museum, content with our aloneness. Both of us dreaded coming home to the memories that awaited us, and to another year without Susie.

⤙⟐⟐⤚

We spend most of our time and energy in a kind of horizontal thinking. We move along the surface of things going from one quick base to another, often with a frenzy that wears us out. We collect data, things, people, ideas, profound experiences, never penetrating any of them...But there are other times. There are times when we stop. We sit still. We lose ourselves in a pile of leaves or its memory. We listen and breezes from a whole other world begin to whisper.

James Carroll

Everybody needs a place to go and recover the core of who they are. A house should be like a mother, it's where you go to heal.

Robert McAlpine

During the spring of 1990, my house became my healing place. There were many days when I did not want to leave its safety and quiet. I realized how it comforted and held me, and one day I acknowledged it, too, was weary and in need of renewal. I had learned from years of being in real estate that houses hold emotion and energy, that they can reflect sadness or happiness.

I decided to paint the interior by myself, with the exception of the high hall spaces, which John painted. I lost myself in the physical task. Unlike working in sales, I could see the physical results of my work. I had a start and finish, and felt comforted as I slowly watched the walls brighten and respond. We installed new counter-tops, wallpaper, and finally carpet; I felt the house appreciated it all. I smiled, remembering Mom's words of advice to a neighbor, who was in emotional pain, "Go do something physical! Paint the side of your garage."

I am grateful for this place that held me as I healed, from which I saw countless sunrises and sunsets. I am very conscious of its moods and shadows. Waking to darkness on a fall morning and padding downstairs to start the coffee. A lamp turned on becomes the center of a golden and comforting circle as it warms the ceiling and casts its shadows.

There's a softness and gentleness to a house in the early morning. The morning light silently reaches through the windows, and slowly, bit by bit, brightens each room. Not yet touched by the sun, the rock wall off the back deck holds the quiet as it supports drapes of ivy. From my office, I see the trees on the horizon bathed in sunlight. It's as if my house and I meditate together. I listen and focus with intention and gratitude. This place holds its own language.

The late afternoon sun casts bright, surreal light on the upstairs bedroom. I look at it bathe the wall and an old chair, and imagine this scene a postcard, caught in time. In the past, I seldom gave myself the gift of awareness that I now possess.

Morning was my favorite time to write in my journal as I savored the quiet companionship around me. I was learning how much I could hear when I became quiet and listened.

❧

I wrote in my journal about the anniversary of Susie's passing: *The winter months were hard. We celebrated the day of Susie's birth in January, and we wanted to honor her on this day, too. It was the day of her birth into a new life, when we felt her love and communication so strongly. I can only call it her "second birthday."* We spent the evening, communing with her, thanking her, honoring her on this day of her new beginnings. A bright fire warmed the house, candles glowed, and music filled the rooms. We celebrated her spirit and that she IS. The house seemed filled with a deep peace.

❧

The memory of Susie's first snowfall in Oklahoma flowed through me. I had carried her outside and knelt beside her, watching as her face focused on the wonder of falling snowflakes. Like a kitten she had held still and felt the new sensations, then slowly turned and smiled up at me, holding my eyes as we shared this wordless treasure.

CHAPTER 15

GIFTS FROM TEXAS

In the spring of 1990, Kathy Kitchens Lyda called and invited us to be guests of honor at Susie's Class of '85 High School Reunion. I knew John and I wanted to see her friends and classmates again, and to thank them all. When the time came to walk up to the podium, I was trembling inside. I stood before row after row of familiar faces and read what I had written the night before:

"John and I thank you for inviting us to share in your first class reunion and in this celebration of Susie's life; you honor us. Susie, my daughter, taught me much, for she lived with courage, dignity, passion, and real caring and love for her friends, young and old. She taught me that one person, who lives fully and in the moment, makes a difference. She taught me that only unconditional love was acceptable.

"She taught me to let go, and she teaches me still. Susie was not afraid to risk in creating her world. She surely must enjoy seeing her friends reach for their dreams, their stars. And I feel her love and joy in this celebration today, for she adored Texas and she loved you, her friends. I'd like to share a special poem with you. It's called "Edges," and it reminds me of Susie's life."

When we walk to the edge of all the light we have,
And take the step into the darkness of the unknown,
We must believe one of two things will happen.
There will be something solid for us to stand on,
Or we will be taught how to fly.

The kids started applauding, and rose to stand as I made my way to the back of the pavilion. I did not expect this and I stopped in the aisle, without words. I know Susie received and gave love there, for I felt her presence, and many of her friends did too, telling me, "You know, she's here."

I've dreamt in my life
Dreams that have
stayed with me ever
after and changed my ideas: they've gone
through and through me,
like wine through water,
and altered the
color of my mind.
Emily Bronte

⇥⋈═◯═⋈⇤

At the reunion, one of Susie's grade-school friends gave us a big hug. We smiled that her mannerisms were so much the same. She stood close and asked if she could talk with me.

We walked to a quiet spot and she said, "One night, a few weeks after Susie died, she appeared to me." She took a deep breath. "I was in my bedroom and turned around and Susie was there."

She continued, "She did not say anything, just stood there, smiling her beautiful smile and looking at me, and then she was gone. Nothing like this had ever happened to me before and I will never forget it."

I was touched and delighted to hear about Susie appearing. I said to Susie later, "OK, Susie daughter. You've been busy. But I want to see you too."

⇥⋈═◯═⋈⇤

A young man who had a near-death experience approached us, "I came close to death and had a vision. I assure you your daughter is with loved ones." Another friend hugged on us and said, "At the memorial service I could see Susie moving down the aisle with her hands held out, saying, 'Don't be sad.... I am here!'"

Our return to Texas gave us more gifts that we could ever have anticipated. Kathy and I met for lunch the next day. This delicate and beautiful young woman remains a joy to us.

Gazing at me across the restaurant table, she said, " One week before Susie died, late at night, I was awakened out of sleep. Susie was sitting on the foot of my bed, looking at me." (At that time, Susie was in Washington with us.)

"Susie said, 'Kathy, I have to go, but I can't leave until you let me go. Everything is going to be all right.' I sat up in bed and argued with her, 'I don't want you to go. Please don't go.' And Susie said, 'I have to go. Everything will be all right. You have to let me go.'"

I remembered the love Susie felt for this friend, and wondered at the soul connection we have with others. It was because of Kathy and Robert that Susie was able to live independently as long as she did in the small house by T.C.U. Susie told me how Kathy would help her up the stairs when she felt ill, how Kathy checked on her, how Kathy loved her. And now I was hearing about a connection, a love between two young women that honored them both.

Kathy later became Director of Cancer Education for Harris Methodist Health System, and wrote, "Sometimes I find while doing the work I do now that I am daily influenced by Susie. I'm not sure why I am here yet, but I know there is a reason and she has something to do with it." In 1998 she founded Camenae Group, Inc., a health-education and physician management company.

Before we flew home I received a phone call from another of Susie's friends. This friend simply told me he had seen Susie the week after she left. Susie appeared to him one night, dressed in a beautiful long gown of gold that shimmered and glowed. She looked healthy and beautiful, with golden hair. Susie radiated love and joy, smiled at him and stayed for a moment, then faded from his sight.

I held the phone, stunned that two men, in separate states, had seen Susie in a similar long, golden dress. He was startled when I told him someone in Seattle had also seen Susie in such a dress, during her service there. And I was swept away that he had shared this gift with me. It was true, I was not being allowed to doubt my daughter's existence or her spirit.

Later, I received a note from my friend Audra in Texas, her compassion coming across the miles. *"Death is the end of a life, it's not the end of a relationship."*

We all have our own connection to that invisible part of us. There is much more to life than simply living out our days as form, then disappearing into an abyss of infinite nothingness. Our thoughts are a magic part of us, and they can carry us to places that have no boundaries and no limitations. In that dimensionless world of thought everything is possible.

Wayne Dyer, *You'll See It When You Believe It*

Formal Christmas party, 1984.

CHAPTER 16

REFLECTIONS IN A MIRROR

I learned with my daughter that "support" was not about me, my wants and wishes but about supporting her on her path, her learning, her experiences, honoring her, and seeing later that her footprints had purpose and meaning. It was watching the wind blow the sand and finding treasure after treasure.

My memories were full of Susie's determined actions and spirit. I remembered her last summer when Robert mailed her a plane ticket. She flew back to Texas and moved into an apartment with him. She called and told us, her voice asking us to understand; we did. We were just exhausted and did not know what else to do.

The phone ringing, from concerned people in Texas: "You let her come back down here?" (Let her?) "Your daughter is very sick, and you're going to regret time not spent with her."

"Mom," she would tell me, "I had to go. Please understand. I will be back soon."

A phone call from a friend: "Mollie, I had to call and see how you are. People are saying that you are having a nervous breakdown, that you are rejecting Susie."

I was appalled and saddened that people could even think these thoughts.

We never "rejected" our daughter, although to some people that must have sounded like good drama. We could not treat Susie as if she was a child, for she wasn't, and she would have none of it. I would be amazed when some people would talk about "making" her do something. Did they know my daughter?

A huge lesson I have learned with my daughter's journey is that other people's judgments are not mine, although they may seem to be totally directed at me. Their fears and reactions are theirs, despite how personal they can feel. Constantly under stress, I was being asked to hold my center, my truth.

⋄→══⊙⊙══←⋄

From my journal: *I can't have people bring their fear into my life. Fear consumes. It blocks life and it blocks love. I have to keep releasing my fears, surrendering, asking for help on handling this, to keep knowing my Knowing. So I will block people who are full of fear, for I, too, am fearful, and their anxieties feed mine. I fight to stay open to the whispers of what is really happening. I want God to pick me up and tell me it will be all right, that Susie will stay here. I pray with all my being for her to stay. This is not a time for fear.*

In her better moments during her intensive chemo treatment, Susie and I talked about how she had used her anger, and that some people were mad at her Dad and me for "deserting" her and not doing things differently.

She said, "I know I used my anger against you and Dad, but that is between us, and I am the one who wanted to stay in Texas and have my own life." Then she said something that sank in. "Mom, most of those people who are criticizing you and Dad haven't invited me over or offered to help me. They are reacting to my cancer and staying outside of it."

I let her words "staying outside of it" come into me.

After Susie left we learned on a deeper level that people in this culture do not want to acknowledge death. Many steadfastly avoided any mention of our daughter - or that we had even experienced parenthood. I often found myself protecting their feelings, making room for their fears, swallowing my voice, my reality. Only with John and a handful of close friends could I be open. I was hugely aware of the barrier created by our reality, and of the silent world we now inhabited.

I feel indignant about this part of my life being denied to me, and treated as though it were "untouchable." I wrote in my journal, "Do you with children love to talk about your children? Just because mine is no longer here does not mean that I am different. I am a mother. My daughter lived fully and well, with joy and passion. Do not act as if she did not exist, for she did and she does. You do and you always will."

I have been here since the beginning and I shall be until the end of days, for there is no ending to my existence.

Kahlil Gibran

A dream in February 1991: *I could go to Susie, although she was in a large square-looking box with invisible walls. I could approach and she could come out of the box and visit with me. We loved being with each other, our souls knowing the other so well. There was a gentle, strong person sitting outside a corner of the box, looking after her. It is so very good to be with her. I am drawn like a moth to flame.*

My day is full of memories and dreams of Susie, but I have to be careful about sharing my thoughts. People know how to grieve and cry at a death but they are at a loss to handle the aftermath. Either they shy away from confronting their own feelings, or they do not know what to say. How many times do we look at someone and fear that we might be looking in a mirror? We fear anger and signs of feelings. We fear tears, which are so necessary and cleansing. "I didn't mean to make you cry."

In *Women Who Run With the Wolves*, Estes writes: *Tears are a river that takes you somewhere. Weeping creates a river around the boat that carries your soul-life. Tears lift your boat off the rocks, off dry land, carrying it down river to someplace new, someplace better.*

Do not fear and shun me, for I have read in your eyes, "You are my biggest fear." You isolate me with your fears and your beliefs. We look at something like this as a disaster, but there was nothing about Susie that was a disaster, her living or her transition to another world or existence. The message we receive from our youngest years onward is that death is to be feared; we grow up fearful and learn early to avoid facing our mortality.

→⊱⊰← ⊱⊰←

I marveled that John could be so strong and steadfast, when I knew how much he was hurting; he was isolated with his grief. We often felt bewildered that this was our reality. We supported each other as best we could, being kind and loving friends when we had energy for nothing else.

It can be lonely, especially for a man in this culture, to lose a child and be isolated because no one wants to talk about it. Instead of feeling supported, men are often abandoned to deal with their grief in silence.

John needed to voice his grief with someone whom he did not have to worry about protecting. He needed his own place and eventually found it when he was ready. I often told him, "You deserve to be heard, you deserve to have your feelings honored, you deserve support."

A friend said to me years later, "It's as if people feel there is a black cloud over your head and they don't want to get anywhere near that shadow, in case it touches them." As if some flaw existed, some curse.

We badly needed a change, to get away from the familiar.

Whidbey Island, a beautiful wooded island in Washington's Puget Sound, became an important healing place for us. There, we bought an old house overgrown with blackberry bushes and encroaching woods. John spent many weekends working on the house and tearing down piles of brush and burning them. The solitude and physical labor helped him work out his grief, and I watched as his health slowly improved. We often ended the day together in silence, watching the sun set on the mountains and the large freighters moving silently up and down the Sound.

One fall day, I wrote in my journal, *I am at Whidbey Island, sitting in the woods on a fallen tree. In front of me is a stately old tree with ivy growing up its trunk. Some of its knobby roots lift from the earth and reach in all directions, looking primeval and territorial.*

It is fall and half of the golden leaves have fallen from the tree. The leaves are positioned up and down the limbs as if for a reason. Some are close to the mother trunk as if they need reassurance and closeness. Others near the end of the branches seem to yearn to touch the sky.

Each leaf falls with its own dance, its own uniqueness. The tree is calm and the leaves remind me of people mindful of manners, this is your turn, your moment. One drops and spins in slow motion to earth. Another, close to the mother source, tumbles, spins quickly to its destiny.

The ground below is a carpet thick with golden leaves, some already dry, curling this way and that. The freshly fallen ones glow with their color and life force. Four leaves drop at the same time, from about the same height, as if they have agreed to share this moment.

The woods are musical with the sounds of birds talking, and squirrels and of leaves dropping in the dusk.

·▸‖══◉ ◉══‖◦·‖

Your pain is the breaking of the shell that encloses your understanding.

Kahlil Gibran

Our inner world and perspective were now different, never to return to yesterday. When we grieved, we were reeling from the pain of separation and needed the comfort of others. But I found myself claiming aloneness, for I often felt clumsy around people. My mind and body quickly tired. What could I say without giving voice to my pain, my despair, my anger?

As months went by, John and I kidded one another that we seemed to have the capability of "clearing a room." If we mentioned our daughter's "death," people would disappear; it happened again and again, to our mixed emotions.

People looked at us when we gathered socially, and they often felt awkward talking about their children in front of us. We, now outsiders, remembered poignantly the deep satisfaction of watching our child in special moments. Others, upset about an incident with their child, may have glanced into our eyes and realized what their world could be. We were, and are, a constant reminder that their worst dreams are capable of manifesting.

Once, we went to a friend's house for a small gathering. A woman sat down next to me and spoke about her children and all they are involved in, and then asked me, "Do you have children?"

I struggled for words.

"Our daughter passed away a year ago."

I watch her eyes shut down. She excused herself and moved away, and did not approach me again that evening.

At a dinner, people talked about a young woman who'd been in an accident and whose face would be scarred despite plastic surgery. One father intently said, "Can you imagine anything worse?" They know our loss and I try to keep my balance in this moment, feeling disbelief, searching for John's eyes.

"Yes," I said, I can imagine worse."

On another occasion, a woman without children asked me, "Are you over it yet?"

I look at her, trying to fathom the question.

Someone asks at a social gathering if I have children. I say, "I had a fabulous daughter, who is still fabulous, but no longer here." A grocery checker asks about kids, and I smile and say, "Two. Both gone from home."

Flying back from our second Christmas spent in England, I sat next to an Englishwoman then living in Canada. She asked me, "Do you have children?"

I took a deep breath and answered, "Yes, a wonderful stepson, Todd, who lives in Texas, and a beautiful daughter, who has passed on."

She looked fully at me and asked, "How did you handle it?" She really wanted to know!

I felt brought in from the cold. The experience was so unusual it became memorable.

⇢➤❖❂⇠

My women's group was a lifeline for me. In my journal, I wrote: "Reine usually leads a meditation, and then we talk about whatever comes up. In the quiet and safety we often gain insights into our lives. I am grateful when someone picks up on Susie's energy; her presence is often felt when we gather, and I feel she enjoys these gatherings.

It was often with these friends that I found a safe haven and support during my daughter's last year and her new beginnings. Reine accepted us with gentle wisdom and humor, "Oh, you're not perfect yet?"

One of my friends in the group, Susan McDaniels, came over one evening and said, "Talk to me about Susie." It was so welcome. We ended up with picture albums in our laps, sitting on the floor, drinking wine, laughing and shedding tears, memories alive with the sharing. I felt I had been handed a precious gift.

⋅⊱⋅▬◉◯▬⋅⊰⋅

The mention of my child's name
may bring tears to my eyes
but it never fails to bring
music to my ears.
Nancy Williams

⋅⊱⋅▬◉◯▬⋅⊰⋅

Sue, whose son died several years ago, said many friends had passed out of her life while new ones had entered. She said she often felt a sense of isolation from the world moving around her. I looked at her and knew what she was saying.

We felt somewhere along the line, we had missed a step, and a blanket of cold reality separated us from what once was. Some days flowed with ease, but other times we worked to keep the missing and pain at bay. I hugged my friend, and she said,

"I was fine, until I saw you."

I told her, "You are fine now and so are your tears."

"But not in public," she said.

And I said, "Yes, in public." This day was her son's birthday and the missing moved through her.

I sought my inner quiet and accepted my intuition. I felt his presence and warming love around her, knowing she was finding her way. I hugged my friend, grateful that we had touched each other's lives.

⋅⊱⋅▬◉◯▬⋅⊰⋅

I heard of a young woman, Tammy, who attended the University of Texas and had been diagnosed with cancer. She was having a hard time with her friend's reactions. I asked for her phone number and called her.

Her spirit impressed me immediately as she told me about her illness and her friends. I told her, "This is a time of change and courage." She would lose friends, for some people would not be able to handle her illness, and she should remember that this was about them and not her. When Tammy's friends saw her, they confronted their own fears and shadows. I said, "It's growing time and there are many blessings ahead."

Later, I called her mom and could only smile when she told me that many people were critical about the way she and her husband "handled" their daughter during this crisis.

Since then, I've received calls from doctors, counselors, or friends who refer parents and young adults to me. Their request is the same, "I was wondering if you would call…."

And I call because I'm glad when I can help in any way. I listen to their fear, pain, anger, and hope. No one tells them about the surprises that come with life-threatening illness; the chaotic anger, the need for independence, the friends who cannot stay.

I remember corresponding with Laura, a young AIDS patient. She wrote me, "I was blessed with a warning from God. He wanted to make sure I enjoyed every day and everything around me that He created. Finding out what I had didn't give me a death sentence, it gave me a life sentence. And I'm living it more now than I ever have."

Many times I receive calls in return.

"Thank you for what you said to me," the caller would say.

"It helped me prepare."

Yes, my arms swing wide sometimes, feeling compassion for this whole experience.

CHAPTER 17

EACH STEP WE TAKE

All goes onward and outward,
Nothing collapses.
And to die is different
From what anyone supposed
And luckier.
      Walt Whitman, "Song of Myself"

More than a year after Susie "transitioned," I was strongly drawn to visit a local intuitive and asked for communication from our daughter.

The intuitive began talking, "Susie is doing very well where she is. She's very happy with things. She wants very much to convey to you that she is extremely happy. She says, 'Mom, I'm home. I'm really home. I'm happy being home.'"

I listened, with tears rolling down my face, as I felt Susie's spirit and this truth.

The intuitive continued with Susie's message. "I knew – I knew in myself that there were ways of moving beyond the cancer, with my mind. I knew that, but you see, I had to come home."

I thought of my recurring dream, "It's of the mind. You can heal." I remembered the times when I had felt turning points, choices being made.

Susie's message went on, "I had to come into this life for several reasons. One was that I had to know if I could move in this reality. Before I came, I was told I had sensitivity and intuitiveness that would stay with me and sometimes would not support me. But I had to come and see if I could help people accept the love, the spirit and the joy inside of themselves."

She said, "I have not come often to this dimension. My worlds are otherworldly or other planetary. You must know it's not a tragedy, what happened. I wanted to try - I did my best and you did your best. I knew I could cure it, but there was no point, for I couldn't cure my inability to work with the density of the earth plane. I want you to know I couldn't have chosen better than to be with you, and I continually send you love and support."

She finished, "You know, we've just changed form. I am still your daughter. I love you."

I went home that day, overwhelmed with this closeness, this acknowledgement of our relationship and the countless mysteries of life, and filled with Susie's presence and her communication to me.

·→►⊫⊜⊨◄←·

I remember vividly communicating with her when she was a baby, and having to remind myself to use words. Gradually, I learned to quiet my mind and body so that I could hear more clearly. Mostly I would feel Susie's presence and telepathically talk with her. I was very grateful for what I received, but it was frustrating to want more than our mostly silent communication. I wanted to see and hear Susie.

In the late summer, John and I drove up to Lake Katchis in the mountains to spend the afternoon. We hiked the trails and then spread a blanket in our special spot overlooking the stream. We sat silently, enjoying the sound and tranquility and meaning of this place. I thought, "an overwhelming sense of love surrounds us," and then I felt Susie's presence.

She was standing to the side, just beaming down at her parents, her "parentals." I smiled, feeling the blessing, and said, "Honey, she's here."

Once again, my breath caught as John pointed toward her "presence".

"She's standing over there, smiling and loving on us," he said.

My cup could not feel any fuller at that moment, the sun and breeze gentler or this bewildering life more sweet. Thank you, Susie. Thank you, Swope. What a daughter we have.

·→►⊫⊜⊨◄←·

I was drawn to study crystals, deeply curious about their presence in my dreams and also Susie's experiences. I would hold a stone and try to receive any thought or emotion that came to me. Then I would look it up in a book, to see what it metaphysically claimed to represent. I was amazed at how often it reflected what I had thought or felt. Crystals, many believe, reflect the emotional, mental and body spectrum. It became an exercise in intuition and a way to focus on receiving the unspoken, an inner voyage of sorts.

Once, I took six different stones with me when we visited relatives. Our nephew, Alex, was about three. During a quiet moment, I asked him

to sit with me and hold the stones.

With all his childhood innocence and intuition, he held each one in his small hand and thoughtfully described its properties, accurately. He held a citrine, known for clarity, and pointed to his head, "My head wants to think." He held a hematite, known for grounding and calming, and pointed to the grass outside the den door. He held a rose quartz, patted his chest, and said, "Hugging my Mom." He expanded my world that day.

⊶⊷◉⊷⊶

In the spring of 1990, John and I were strongly drawn to visit the restaurant where Susie worked as a waitress before moving back to Texas. It had been too hard to go before, with the place full of our memories of watching her as she laughed and worked.

For some reason, on that weekend we were meant to go. As we were seated, the waitress handed us a menu, and we found ourselves looking at a picture of Susie and three other people on the cover. Susie was standing to one side and the others across from her, divided by the large vertical words, "Enjoy."

I could not speak as I looked at my smiling daughter. John and I were both stunned. "That's Susie!"

I asked the waitress if I could have a menu, and she said, "Sure, we're replacing these with new menus tomorrow."

Another gift from Susie. In the photo, now framed on my den wall, Susie is standing alone, as if on her separate path. And the word dividing her from the others is "Enjoy." The impact of that day, the timing of our being drawn there and receiving this affirmation is still amazing to us. I look at this gift, another reminder that she IS, and smile.

⊶⊷◉⊷⊶

Another time, we spent a weekend on the Oregon coast and were returning home a different way than usual. We nearly passed a weathered barn-like building with an artist's sign, but were strongly drawn to stop. Upon entering, we saw a lovely older woman, a huge dog and an old man who reminded me of Picasso. The walls and tables were covered with abstract art and classical music filled the air.

John and I wandered around the room, admiring the artist's works. Then the old man approached, introduced himself as Dodson, quietly looked at us and said, "What happened to you?"

Shaken, I managed to say after a moment, "Our daughter passed away," and my tears came. I struggled to regain my composure, wondering how and what he knew.

Still looking at us, "I want you to choose a print. It is my gift to you."

We tried to refuse but he was insistent and we finally chose one that moved us. "Ah," he said, "so you picked that one...I will tell you about it."

He told us that several years ago he was attacked, beaten and nearly died. When he recovered, he painted this passionate work, filled with light and dark, to celebrate his survival and life. He named it, "Heartbeat...I exist...I am alive." Perhaps, I thought, I was in a time warp having an amazing experience in an amazing old building and I would wake up soon.

We knew we were in the presence of spirit and being supported and loved. It was a message of a life enduring earthly storms, delivered to us in yet another unexpected way. We proudly display our art, still feeling the wonder and mystery of that encounter.

·⤖⊶·

One day, a friend dropped by and left a rose bush on the porch. A card read, "John, Mollie, and Susie. May the roses live with her sunny memories, and the yellow symbolize the roses of Texas."

We chose a spot for it, and John carefully planted it. Each spring, we watch it leaf out and produce the most luxurious yellow, cream and pink roses. We call it Susie's Rose Bush, and bless our friend for her thoughtful gift.

Then, on my birthday, my artist friend Diane gave me a beautiful painting of roses. It was exactly like the rose left on our porch, which Diane had never seen.

"Diane," I said one day, "Come with me."

I took her outside to show her the roses, blooming almost in exact replication of the painting. She and I stood silent, amazed and once more I silently gave thanks for all the small miracles in my life. This world is not allowing me to feel alone.

·⤖⊶·

Another time, a friend Sara brought me a gift in the form of a Chilean coin. On it was an angel with her hands and arms reaching upwards, wings spread full. It reminded me of the picture of Susie with her arms and face embracing the sky. I pulled it from my purse and showed it to my friend, both of us silent in the moment. It was another affirmation and I could feel Susie's delight at our connection.

My sister, Susan, wrote: *This existence of ours is absurdly painful at times, sometimes for months or years at a stretch. We live in a place of such profoundly beautiful mental, visual, audio and sensory stimuli that it is a shame we humans can't just live in that positive realm. I don't have to stretch my imagination very much to think everything beautiful here is one dimension of heaven.*

Over time, many people responded to the news of Susie's illness and leaving by saying to me, "Such a tragedy," or "How very tragic for you all." I know their words were heartfelt and kind, but after deep reflection I came to the realization that the words did not fit. *Words are powerful, holding meaning and intent.*

When it happened next, I gently looked at my friend and said, "Susie's leaving was the unthinkable, but there was nothing about her life or her leaving that is a tragedy. She did it too very well for me to be able to use that word." My friend looked at me and nodded her understanding.

For three years after Susie left, I experienced a physical presence and silent communication. This was one of the reasons I craved being quiet, in my house, without a world full of noise and confusion. I would not feel her around for periods of time. But she always came back, and John and I would know it. She still does. Sometimes he will speak first, "Susie was with me today."

I could hear the whispers across the barrier that separated us, could feel her close, and could feel myself dance around the room, both of us laughing, as we did when she was growing up. She was reminding me and I was learning that the barriers we accept as a "given" in this lifetime can be pushed aside.

We on earth are used to loud messages, raised voices, "This is the truth," but it is not so heavy handed. It can be whispers and body-felt knowings. So much communication comes in quiet moments, when the mind and body are not resisting and arguing, but relaxed and flowing. We know the ease we feel after a long walk, slow breathing or meditating. We must ask to surrender into this feeling, this sensation.

We want our communication to be as solid as the body, as loud as the voice, but we must learn that we are often sent fragments and whispers. These can suddenly burst into silent confirmation as a whole. We finally see the pieces have an individual and collective purpose. I believe Susie wants to teach people that there are not the endings we imagine.

Love does not end, just the body. I wanted Susie "here," but I fiercely appreciated and honored what I had with her. There were days when the pleasure of knowing our bond was like a blanket over my missing. I will own what I have. It is enough, in this moment, in this now.

In valuing the mind as much as we do, we have a tendency to deny mystery, to deny the spiritual.

Rachel Naomi Remen, *Noetic Sciences*

CHAPTER 18

YOU WERE HERE TODAY

There are no unnatural or supernatural phenomena, only very large gaps in our knowledge of what is natural. We should strive to fill those gaps of ignorance.
Astronaut Edgar Mitchell

Eddie called, "I hope this doesn't sound crazy, but how is Susie?" No, it did not sound crazy; it was the most wonderful thing I had been asked in a long time. My friend was asking about Susie, as if this was my norm and gifting me with her knowing that my daughter IS.

I savored my reply. "Eddie, thank you so much for asking. I know she's doing great, but I haven't felt her presence in the last couple of months."

She asked, "What do you think she's doing?"

I said, "I only know that she feels far away in some kind of intensive learning, and that she will be back soon." I was so grateful she would ask. This conversation felt real and sane. I was thankful to have a friend who would call and ask me such a question.

Sometimes when I was missing Susie, I would call Reine to see what she felt Susie was doing. Without fail, she would sense Susie to be close, around John or I, with other people, in a learning atmosphere or far away. And I would be feeling the same. I craved confirmation of my intuitive communication with my child. It was so very good to talk about my daughter and how she was, what she was doing, even though she was no longer here in "earth body." *I am still a mother.*

⊶══◉═══⊷

A friend wrote, *I stood in awe when I visited you two while she was in the hospital. I've never seen such strength and courage come from within a person. She set an example for us all. You did a lot of right things in raising Susie because she was indeed a blessing to everyone she came in contact with.*

⊶══◉═══⊷

I wrote in my journal: *When I think of Susie, I feel her creating part of our connection. She has taught me how to listen and receive. She comes into my mind for a certain reason, to be with me, to share something. This barrier between us is like slipping into water — still my same body but a different sensation, perception. A clarity of intuition and lessening of the awareness of time and matter, the physical. There is too much fear on this earth about having and leaving the body, about our existence. I want to help change that perception. I know Susie does.*

Though cancer overwhelmed her physical body, she taught me that our spirits endure in an ever-changing universe and we truly are more than we can perceive or understand at this time. Susie's transition and the years that followed have taught me to not fear death. She is quite an insistent teacher – my daughter.

I often feel her happiness with the element she now inhabits. In my thoughts and meditations, she wants me to be aware of how quickly and easily she can move, how instantly her energy is manifested. She is in another form but still very much a part of this life. A friend wrote, "She's just living somewhere else."

In the spring of 1993, I experienced another transition with Susie, and since then I have had less physical presence of her and more a thought, or telepathic relationship. And less a mother-daughter relationship, more one of friendship.

That late winter my body and heart grieved, and I wrote in my journal that I knew I was being asked to "let go." I did not understand it, but I felt a deep sadness and loss, a tearing separation, and pain in my back, neck, and arms. I could not understand my angst, yet knew it was a time of powerful change. I wrote, "I am willing to follow my path, and honor Susie's. But this really feels awful."

·-»»»·◉ ◉»«·

A Dream: *Susie had come for a visit. It was now time for her to go and we were on a wide sidewalk on a bridge over railroad tracks. Somebody who would do harm approached and was threatening me. Susie ran up and kicked him, distracted him, and we were then safe. I couldn't see Susie. I ran to the bridge railing and looked down and there she was, running along on the platform, many tracks below. I leapt over the railing and landed safely in front of her and grabbed her into my arms. "You're all right," I said. She was crying and a little frantic because she needed to leave and return to the other side and she had missed the opportunity. She was running to find another 'window' to the other side. I said, "I'll take you there...I wouldn't leave you now." She relaxed into my arms, comforted.*

We were next in the Texas hill country amongst some big boulders, an endless sky and vistas. I put Susie down, knowing this was a 'permanent' window where she could come and go at will. I hugged her and thanked her for coming. There was tremendous clarity for her here, clear frequencies. She approached and disappeared into the rocks.

·-»»»·◉ ◉»«·

A note from Eddie:
Memories flood over me, us, all of us, in waves and in tiny vignettes. Susie's passing (her transition) is victorious for her, lonely for those left behind. But what footprints she left. I have her picture and yours, taken in a wooded clearing. The three of you are sitting on a picnic table - 1987 - yesterday, and at the same time eons ago.

⭒

In May, 1993, I visited an intuitive teacher. I first asked about Susie, not telling the intuitive what I had been experiencing.

She immediately said, "My friend, Susie has transitioned. She sends you tremendous love, but she no longer wears the form she did. She wants to communicate with you, not on the daughter-mother level, but as an equal."

The intuitive went on, "She has transitioned to another dimension, but the telepathic communication you share will continue. She wants to communicate through you and to you, but the level of physical contact you felt with her will not be the same as in the past.

"She too is growing and evolving, but be assured, you and she will always be connected and communicate in this lifetime."

That was what my body and spirit were grieving, without my conscious knowledge of what was happening.

On Mother's Day, unaware of all this, Reine sent me a mother's day card, "from Susie," that said. "To Mom, a very special friend." She said she had been drawn to get that card and send it to me. "Susie told me to...."

One of Susie's friends, Jennifer, told me an adventure they had. "When Susie was in the heart of sickness, we dressed to kill and went out. We had more fun! Susie was determined to get me a man." She then said, "Mollie, she sits on our shoulders and will always be part of our lives." Friends have called or written me to say, "I really felt Susie with me today."

April, whom Susie loves, one day felt Susie with her very strongly, admonishing her to be careful and concentrate on her driving. She went home and told her mother that Susie had helped her. A manifestation of strong thought, or was it communication from the "other side?"

⭒

You were here today-
I heard your laughter in the plaza
I saw your hope in a patient's eyes
I've missed you my friend...
But you were here today.

Kathy Kitchens Lyda

·⊶≡◉≡⊷·

In 1996, Rachel wrote me that she had dreams about Susie. I asked her if she would share any of them with me.

She wrote: *After I wake up and remember my dream, I feel like she's checked in on me. Other dreams are sometimes difficult to remember, but the ones with Susie never are, because the feelings I have during the dreams are so powerful. I remember the feeling of love more than the dream itself. And later on in the morning, I always have a very strong longing feeling along with my delight at having her there.*

But the breakthrough I've had is that we were alone this time and she let me tell her everything I wanted to and didn't, before she left. It was the most incredible thing, because it wasn't like any other dream, not a possible recreation of something that had actually happened. This was a dream that seemed to be taking place in the present.

Part of my pain was feeling guilty about not telling her so many things that I should have. She helped me by giving me another chance to tell her. She's still showing love and concern to me, and she's doing it from another place!

·⊶≡◉≡⊷·

A dream in December, 1993:

John and I are in a tall, airy room with big windows. Susie appears, just as solid as we are. We're thrilled to see her — she looks beautiful, healthy, telling us, "Yes, I'm here!"

I see a bed frame, and there is a small bright point of light in it that glows and grows bigger. I kneel down. Susie is very tiny and sitting within the opening of light. Her hand reaches out and she sprinkles me with blue crystal dust, then hands me a green stone that glows. We smile at each other.

Now we are with a group of friends, and I put my hand on her cheek and say, "If only I could see you like this just once a month." She changes her form and is flying around the room, gracefully floating near the ceiling on her back, then gently turning and floating elsewhere. She tells me she has to leave, her energy to be here is wearing out. She looks so confident and happy. She leaves us, but we know we will meet again.

·⊶≡◉≡⊷·

A dream in 1998: *I am with a group of wise ones who tell me the purpose and essence of this life. I understand it so clearly and feel their presence but cannot remember their words when I awake. I know it was about loving and not judging or limiting ourselves to the physical. It was about learning to see beneath or beyond the external, almost as if exercising an aspect of our spirit, honing it. Seeing endless perspectives and wonders on this beautiful planet, knowing we visit this place and create here with our choices and intent. We come to learn about wisdom, our power, our minds and hearts, in this element. There is much learning available through the body.*

Limitations, emotional and physical experiences are the catalyst to growth and spiritual awakening, by their very physical reality. But the essence of it is to learn about love on this level — to love, and to know we are not separate but are all connected.

I wake from this dream knowing something profound has been given me, trying to remember it all. I accept the pieces I have retained as enough for now.

-◦>══◉ ◉══<◦-

The most beautiful thing we can experience is the mysterious.
                                                                    Einstein

CHAPTER 19

THAT KIND OF ATTENTION

Seeing death as the end of life is like seeing the horizon as the end of the ocean.
David Searls

The realization sinks deep that no one loves you, regards you, as does your child. There is a tremendous gift in that. I knew that never again would anyone give me *that kind of attention.* The words, "Never again," had run through my mind, over and over, when my mother passed on, and now I felt their finality once more.

The loss of my mother and the loss of my daughter. I miss them both. Two such powerful women in my life. In my bedroom, I have a picture of my mother, and above that a picture of my daughter. Between them is a framed card that a friend sent me after Susie left:

To every thing
there is a season
and a time
to every purpose
under the heavens
Ecclesiastics

⊰⊱

I had realized years earlier with Mother and now again, that our unseen loved ones give and give to us. Expect the unexpected, and try not to be fixated on the form in which communication and gifts are sent. They may have to wait until we are asleep or very quiet inside, but we receive. In this world of constant change and seasons, we can open ourselves to this gift. You will know when you have been touched.

⊰⊱

I hold a piece of paper with Susie's handwriting:
"As we stare off into space, some of us are able to map out our dreams, while others are lost among the stars. Don't let yourself be one of the lost stars."

Today, we celebrate Susie's 31st birthday. I awakened to a vivid dream: *Susie was in high school and I was visiting her at the school. I saw her and no one else. We were so happy to see one another. I walked quickly, and I reached her we embraced. I felt her body, smelled her hair as it brushed my face, and felt her joyful spirit. We stood together, holding each other, full with love. Then she looked into my eyes and I knew she had to go elsewhere. She was healthy and happy. The dream was so real and clear. No words were spoken.*

Rachel called that night and said, "Happy Birthing Day." She knew Susie always greeted me with this on her birthday. Rachel's own birthday is tomorrow, another connection these two friends shared. She has dreams of Susie too, without words, but words are not needed.

In September of 1996, my friend, Jerri Davis, and I were in Washington, D.C. for a University of Washington "Human Rights Seminar." One day we decided to enjoy a glass of wine at the Mayflower Hotel. I was strongly drawn to move to the other side of the room from where we originally sat. In a little while, a woman approached and asked if she could join us. She said she was a lobbyist for alternative medicine. I told her I was very interested because of my daughter, who had passed on. I did not describe Susie to her.

We talked some more. Then she paused and said, "A beautiful being with golden hair is behind your left shoulder. She is like a guardian angel to you. She is very powerful and joyful, her skin a little darker than yours (as Susie's skin was). She is involved in many things, and you and she are very connected. She is with you a lot. She is very powerful, a wonderful spirit, full of light."

I patted my silent friend on the knee. "How are you doing, Jerri?"

My friend smiled with her quiet wisdom. It was so special to share this moment with Jerri, for incidents like this had often occurred after my daughter's passing, and I viewed them as gifts. I pulled photos of Susie from my purse and handed them to the woman, who looked intently and nodded her head.

I was full of gratitude and the wonder of the moment.

Everyone takes the limits of his own vision for the limits of the world.
Arthur Schopenhauer

It is a strange thing to be without someone who was immensely important in your life. They are physically gone, but remain a presence and are influential in countless ways.

A friend urged me to attend a support group for parents who have lost children. I sat in a room heavy with emotion and looked at the faces of those quiet people. I listened as they shared their losses and their pain. There were a few grief stricken parents who had lost a child five or six years ago. There were two women who were very angry and bitter. These were parents whose children had passed away through suicide, accident, or illness.

Listening, I was again overwhelmed by the "what ifs," the regrets, the enormous guilt that parents carry. I shared the missing of my daughter, but mostly I listened to them. So much grief and so many people captive in their pain. The world continues on, yet a grieving person feels their world has stopped, and in many ways it has. I realized again the enormous need for forgiveness and love - for our children and ourselves - as the door to healing.

I felt their children wanted them to acknowledge more than the pain. As they spoke the young people became present for me. Did they not have a sense of the whole lives of their children? After two hours, and toward the end of the meeting, I said, "I know how much it hurts when our children leave us." I struggled to find words. *Not once have I heard a joyful story about your children, or gratitude that they were in your lives. I am so grateful for the knowing of my daughter. Our children's lives must be celebrated and honored, not just grieved.*

But grieve we do for the enormity of having and missing, however a loved one passes through our lives, however many years pass. We are here to experience our humanity. Grief can come and sit within our body and heart, numbing and shifting our perspective on everything. Somehow, over time I learned there was nothing to do but accept the experience as my known, my reality, my joy and despair. And after all these years, it still comes. I wrote on Susie's birthday week in 2000: "I am emotionally crackling, unable to stop the crying that comes like an ocean tide. Tonight I sit under soft blankets and am filled with the missing. I see little sense in this heartache and can only feel my sorrow that feels so big. I know we are all stronger and more fragile than we know, but I am tired tonight, without insights or wisdom. I miss my daughter in all her glory and humanity. I yearn for her."

I shared the tears of all of us, missing a loved one, and surrendered to the moment, knowing it too, had a place in my life.

⋯⟶⟫⊙⟪⟵⋯

There is a fearlessness that comes when one has faced the worst, a realization that nothing can touch you in that way again. Susie, through her words and actions, asked me to live with love and with courage. Because of her, I was forced me to confront my fears and surrender them. What a gift this has been: opening and opening to life.

With surrender came a greater compassion, a deeper compassion. For with the comprehension of "true support" and honoring another soul's choices, there is a different view and a profound sense of another's path.

The missing of our daughter is still intense, but so is the pleasure of knowing her. It is a gift to have "known the best." I give thanks Susie was here for us to see her bloom into adulthood as a glorious young woman. I realize I could have had so much less time with her. I will always want more, but what I had was magnificent and worthy of gratitude. I continue to quiet my mind and feel the countless gifts of her life.

Kathy and Lance Lyda visit us in Seattle.

I dreamt one night that Susie was emphatically telling me, "Mom, it was just my body!"

"Whoa…" With this, I wake up and tell her, "I happened to love that body of yours, and you being in it." I feel Susie's expressive words and hands explaining to me, "Mom, I see color shows that I can walk into, change my form, enter realms of thought and experience the power… the greatness that when I was on earth I felt and sometimes expressed."

I am aware that she can move with incredible quickness; her thoughts and intentions transport her in different ways. I can feel when she is very far away, and I know when she is close again.

You would know the secret of death. But how shall you find it unless you seek it in the heart of life? For life and death are one, even as the river and the sea are one.

Kahlil Gibran, *The Prophet*

·⟶·⟿⟦⟨⟧⟼·⟵·

A dream, February 2000: *A warm spring day with sunshine. I was working at a festival that ran down a long road, taking tickets for admission. I saw a little girl approach; she was about 4 years old. Her hair was wavy and she was gentle, beautiful, so sweet her soul. I knelt and embraced her, knowing in some way I knew her. She knew me too and nestled her arms around my neck and relaxed into the warmth of my body. I looked up and Susie was there, about 10 or 12 years old. She smiled and said, "I knew you would find her." Looking into my eyes she said, "She is the daughter I would have had if I had stayed. I wanted you to see her." I felt such joy to see Susie, then thought it odd that she was so young (with a child) but knew it didn't matter. I embraced Susie, felt her as I had when she was here. We were next at a lovely park and Susie lay in the grass and the little girl sat in my lap. I rubbed Susie's back as she used to love, and hugged the little one. It was so beautiful being with both of them. Time passed and Susie said she must go and take (her child) to see the festival. She clearly adored the little one. They left and I felt such a loss but grateful.*

·⟶·⟿⟦⟨⟧⟼·⟵·

One of the most healing things I do - is give thanks. When I am grieving or missing Susie, gratitude helps transform the pain. Thanking her and honoring her. "*I am so grateful for the knowing of you.* I love you and feel your smile and joy. I thank you for being in my life, for our bond, for your love and presence. Your Mom loves you. I hold you with all the light and love in my being. Always and forever."

I come home to Laura's words: *There is in the design of the soul a purpose, and when we come into this life, we come with this purpose. We decide what we will do here. We decide on our own experiences. Our lives are more in our own hands than we could imagine.*

Somebody told me one day that Susie was now safe and sleeping, and I said with a smile, "I respect your beliefs, but I must tell you, my daughter is not sleeping." I feel Susie laughing, clapping her hands.

The insights she gained years ago fill my mind and heart: *Mom, he said I might be an astronaut — that in the future I would be studying in space or traveling among the stars.*

EPILOGUE

A BIG CLASSROOM IN THE SKY

One morning I awoke from a dream, quietly amused at my reaction to the realization that life here is not meant to be easy, and *our souls know that*. We grow up with myths and stories, but this beautiful planet is not an easy place. Our experiences serve to expand our perspective but are not who we "are." It seems we live so many different lifetimes in one.

M. Scott Peck, in "The Road Less Traveled," wrote, *Life is difficult. This is a great truth, one of the greatest truths. It is a great truth because once we truly see this truth, we transcend it. Once we truly know that life is difficult, once we truly understand and accept it, then life is no longer difficult. Because once it is accepted, the fact that life is difficult no longer matters.*

My memories are filled with joy and tears, passions and compassion. Accepting the wonders I have experienced only motivates me to encourage others to ask for communication, to become quiet and listen for the whispers and messages that come. I often miss my daughter deeply but have not felt abandoned. For whatever purpose and meaning our connection exists, she has "moved" me to another place.

Susie is about teaching perspectives on life, not death. We change and grow, but we do not end. In this life we are given partial vision, and asked to trust and believe the unknown and unseen. Perhaps that is why learning "here" can be so important, because it asks us to reach beyond the physical. It asks us to be more than we think we are.

Her communication, "Mom, life is so much bigger than you know and so are you," remains with me. I smile and now believe that *we are all courageous to be here.* I seek to push the boundaries of my beliefs and accept that there is much I cannot understand in this lifetime, but surely my spirit remembers its purpose and reason for undertaking this experience.

If I get out of the way of my mind (and will), perhaps I can help support a bigger vision for my life. In this vein, I often use the following affirmation, "I ask to do everything I came here to do and more." I do not have to know "what" in order to honor my soul's path.

Many people comment about the memories that remain when a loved one passes over, but I tell them I have more than memories. I experience presence, humor, and unconditional love. I honor this other world or dimension that we on earth are learning to trust. I wonder about my purpose in this lifetime, and believe that my intuition, my communication between this world and the next, is part of my reason for being.

I think of God as the same potential healing force – an intelligent, loving energy or light – in each person's life. Even scientists are now telling us that energy has intelligence.
Bernie Siegel, *Love, Medicine and Miracles*

-->≡◉◉≡<--

I still seek the answer to the dream that began so long ago about healing and the mind. I now understand that "mind" is in every part of our bodies. Dr. Larry Dossey wrote in *Meaning and Medicine*, "It is our thoughts, conscious and unconscious, the intelligence and memory contained in our body and includes the 'meaning" we attach to it all. A friend said she dreamt of her death and realized, "The greatest travesty is not to use the gifts we have – we are the determiners – we choose to be here or not." In meditation one day, I received, "Susie experienced her creations." The words want to be written, but the next day I read them and my heart rebelled. Is this a bigger truth than I can now understand?

-->≡◉◉≡<--

Sometimes I attended Dr. Warner's cancer support group and always came away inspired, in awe of this large group of people who spoke with such courage and humor. One night I said to them, "You people haven't given up your power." They were positive and had taken control of their lives, including those who would not heal from their illness. It is significant to be with one person who impacts you in such a way, much less a group. I remembered when, after Susie had passed, Dr. Warner called and asked John and me to come to his office. He and his wife, Helen, wanted to know how we were. Their compassion and loving-kindness gave us strength and also gratitude that Susie had been in his care.

John wrote, *Our daughter was very special, and had a tremendous impact on my life. Seldom do we meet people who take life head-on and spread such a powerful light as Susie did. We are amazed at the people we still hear from with such special stories of how she affected their lives.*

Recently, a friend wrote, "You write about your daughter and it is painful to read because I find that kind of loss to be tremendously sad. I haven't felt comfortable enough to ask you about her. But, her spirit fascinates me. She sounds so wise and sweet. When I read what you write about her, I get the strangest images of sunshine and I feel very peaceful. It is the strangest thing really. You always sound so strong and happy when you write about her. I feel a little disappointed that I will never get to meet such a woman. I would love to learn from her."

John and Mollie.

Well, it is true. I love to connect with Susie's energy for she continues to bring me joy and guidance. Perhaps this friend and others can meet her. I believe we have many teachers and they do not have to be here, in order to communicate with us. Another friend wrote, "Susie's destiny was to become a teacher – I love the way she is still here infusing the process with light."

My sister-in-law, Dr. Betsy Swope called, "Yesterday my receptionist came in and out of my office several times, and made a special point of coming back in to ask, 'Who is this?' pointing at Susie's picture. 'She is so beautiful and radiant.'

So you see, Mollie, she is still radiating love.... But then you knew that."

THE EARLY YEARS

A DANCING SUNBEAM

In my childhood, my mother gifted me with knowing that intuition was real, and that there were great mysteries and beauties to life. I was raised to love, not fear, God. Mother taught me God was present in all of nature, animals and people. And to die, she said, was to be born to another life that we could not imagine, as a baby being born could not imagine what having a human body on earth would be like.

The day of my mother's first stroke, when I was in seventh grade, I pressed my face against the screen window in my bedroom and stared into a tree, knowing that something had ended and my life would never be the same. My passionate mother, who had taken her children to art galleries, museums, concerts and plays, bird walks at dawn, fishing, camping trips and moonlight walks on beaches during annual treks to Alabama; this magical mother was disappearing.

"Small strokes" alcoholism and depression slowly took away the mother I adored, and replaced her with an explosively angry "other person" who left me deeply shaken. More and more she was determined to control her families every action, furious when her will was challenged.

I took refuge in books and became a loner, having no close friends in school. I would devour one or two books every weekend, and one night, received an intuitive experience of great clarity. While reading an historical novel set in England, I felt transported there, recognized as familiar the landscape being described, felt the wind and mist on my body, and heard the rhythm of the sea. I could feel 'the' woman struggling to handle a deep pain in her life as she walked by the sea.

At that moment I knew I had lived in another time and place, though I had not been taught about reincarnation. I had glimpsed another life in another time and knew that pain, love and hope existed there too. It was a deeper understanding, mixed with mystery, of how we dream, strive and stumble.

I became aware of often experiencing on two different levels: a deep sorrow for my mother's pain and a compassion of knowing that this life would end but her essence, some part of her would continue. I continued to dread my daily reality, but I had been given a bigger perspective that offered comfort. This "psychic window" experience somehow helped give me strength and compassion for my mother, who could no longer find peace or joy in this life.

One year before she actually passed over, I had a dream that told me she had to leave this existence, to go on. I heard a gentle voice whisper, *There is nothing more to be done. There is too much damage. She has to go on.* I hugged my small mother, knowing this was a truth. I accepted now that my will and prayers would not turn the tide.

In my early twenties I found words to express what I had felt then:

It appears to me impossible that I shall cease to exist, or that this active restless spirit, equally alive to joy and sorrow, should only be organized dust. Surely something resides in this heart that is not perishable…and life is more than a dream.

Mary Wollstonecroft Godwin

⇥⇥⊙⇤⇤

I married young, and at nineteen gave birth to Susan Elizabeth (Susie) on a winter night in 1967 in Tulsa, Oklahoma. I have a vivid memory of a beautiful baby being placed in my arms and a nurse exclaiming, "Oh honey, this is one of the most alert babies I have ever seen!" Groggily, I thought to myself, "What…does that mean?"

When Susie was about six months old, I was awakened in the early hours by a brilliant light and became aware of a tall figure in a white robe, radiating light. I knew it to be a man, although I could not see "him" clearly because of the brilliance and diffusion of the light. I had not imagined such brightness was possible, yet it was gentle, and I looked into it. I was drawn to my knees on the bed and felt a yearning to spiral upward, to be with this light, but I thought, "My baby is here." I was not invited to go, or told anything, just bathed and filled with this loving light.

Still kneeling, my face and hair wet with tears, the beautiful light dissipated. I stumbled to my feet and reached into Susie's crib, which was near my bed. I lifted her small body and held her close. She made soft noises, nestled into my body, and I held her in a rocking chair in the living room until dawn, sharing the experience of the light.

For days and months afterwards, I prayed that the white light would come again, but it never did. Years later, I read about similar white light visitations, but those were usually during near-death experiences. I finally came to believe it was an act of absolute love, a gift and a blessing, which I will never forget.

When my daughter was an infant, I was visited by my mother's spirit while I was at the kitchen sink in my apartment. I felt a sensation behind me, and then a flood of warmth as if I was being embraced by two loving arms. Although I glanced over my shoulder, I knew there was no one behind me, and I stood very still to receive this feeling. My back felt a flush of warmth, then my body, with a loving presence that startled me, felt wonderful. My mother had come to give me her "mother love." I knew her love was reaching through the barrier separating us.

My daughter and I became companions going through life together, both of us full of optimism and a yearning to experience life. I marveled at her beauty, fearlessness and willpower.

Two years old. 1969.

I held her close to me when she was a little child and was often swept with overwhelming pride and wonder. I loved to see the contours of her face, her expressions, the way her hair would move and lie in wisps on her head. I was pulled to run and experience my own young life, but it was her life that preoccupied me and directed my focus. She was my one constant, and she delighted my soul as I gave to her and gratefully received her love and attention in return. My child loved me as no one ever had.

As a mom in my early twenties, I would pick Susie up after work, eager to see her small face light up with a pure, joyful smile as she ran into my arms. I still feel the thrill of those moments when she would wrap her small arms around my neck and lay her head on my shoulder and pat my back. At home, she would ride on my left hip as I cooked and cleaned, and we often danced around the room.

From the first, Susie always claimed her sense of self and I admired her inner direction, determination and courage, while I was sometimes in awe at the willpower of such a small child.

We create our lives, but we also swim in the currents of our past. As she grew, I often reverted to some of the ways in which I was raised, my "known." I felt at times enmeshed in my history with memories of my norm versus a drive to let Susie be herself and feel her own power. I was afraid to honor either her or my own instincts.

My life still moved in and out of chaos and my husband was subject to violence. We separated after a final incident of physical abuse when, for the first time, he turned on our three-year-old daughter who had run to help me.

At the hospital, after the x-rays and examination, the doctors said she might have brain damage. I lay beside her that long night, a vigil of waiting to see if she would be all right. I swore to myself, "No more. It ends here, now."

I made a promise to God that night: I would do whatever it took to change our lives. If God would just let her be all right, I would never put her in harms way again. And she would not live the life I had, with a family at war – I swore she would have a childhood. The words "no more" kept moving through my mind.

⊷⊷⊶⊶

My husband left the house the next day, knowing it was the end of our marriage, but not before Susie, her head swollen and bruised, insisted on approaching him while he sat on the couch. Standing in front of him, holding her baby blanket with one arm, she looked up at him and said simply, "Daddy, I forgive you."

I had not prompted this and I wondered, "Where does this come from?" I was in awe of my small daughter, her dignity and enormous heart.

Susie was my child, my companion, and my friend from her earliest years. Sometimes I felt we were more like sisters than mother and daughter. I had many moments of wonder that I was a mother and that this child was mine.

The end of the 1960s and beginning of the 1970s was an amazing time with change in the air. The radio played "This is the Dawning of the Age of Aquarius," and women wore pink, bright orange and bold flower prints. "Demure" and "proper" were thrown upside down. With hot pants and war protest marches, young people challenged tradition and demanded a new perspective.

This was not like the 1950s or early 1960s, when I had carried white gloves and was taught how to sit and walk "like a lady." Susie rode in the car and flashed the peace sign at people (or the Texas Longhorn symbol, if the car had Texas license plates). The popular Helen Reddy's song, "You and Me Against the World," about her and her child was pretty much how I felt with my daughter. We didn't have family around, but we had each other.

One summer night when Susie was four, we sat on the front steps and I held her in my lap as we looked at the

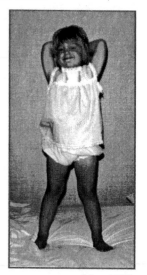

May 1971.

stars filling the sky with their brilliance. We both took a deep breath and sighed together, both of us feeling such contentment.

In the warm weather I called her "Susie Sunshine," and in winter, "Susie Snowflake." At twenty-three, I distinctly remember looking over the neighborhood from my apartment window in St. Louis as the snow was gently falling. I held her close and felt a flood of happiness in the peace of the moment. I had claimed my own life and my own space, and I loved it. If I created stresses or unhappiness within the walls of my home, they were mine. There was no one to depend on to earn a living and take care of my daughter except me.

I met John when Susie was five and a half and I was rather satisfied and content with my life. At the time he was living in Michigan, and had come to St. Louis to visit his family and friends. I had gone to a disco club party with a girlfriend. Looking up, I saw him standing in the doorway with his friend Tom.

He stood out with crystal clarity and everything around him blurred. The room became silent and dim for several seconds, then cleared. (I thought, what is happening...?) He was quite handsome, and I already knew he was special. His eyes met mine across the room and he made his way over to me. Smiling, he introduced himself and asked a very original question, "May I buy you a drink?"

We had a date the following Saturday, to his friend's wedding. He invited me to a pool party the next day, but I told him that I spent Sundays with my daughter. The man definitely hesitated. Then he said, "Why don't you bring her?"

"This could be interesting," I thought.

John and Susie. April 1973.

John knocked on our door the next morning and I let him in. Susie stood quietly back with her hands on her small hips, studying him, checking him out. At the party, they were soon playing and splashing in the pool, while I sunned and watched them. Hmmm.

When he put his arms around me and held me close that night, I heard these words move through me like a gentle wind, "I've come home. I've come home." I felt spooked, "What is happening?" But I knew this man was special in my life.

I think of it now as soul recognition, but we had a lot of earthly stuff to work through. I was possessive with my hard-won independence; I would not consider a relationship with a man who did not love and accept both of us. John did. He moved back to St. Louis and one day came home and said we were getting married. He had arranged the church, the minister and set the date.

We were married in April 1973, with vows we had written ourselves (which included no promises but our commitment of love and respect). We were surrounded by a circle of friends and relatives.

⊷⊷◉⊶⊷

When Susie was seven, we moved to Decatur, Illinois and she entered second grade. Her "sense of self" was as strong as ever. The two of us were driving to the store one day when she blurted, "Mom, I have to be somebody. I can't be like you. (Ouch) I have to BE SOMEBODY."

I could feel her passion and the greatness in her spirit and I loved her fearlessness. This wondrous daughter of mine could take on the world and yet be devastated by seeing the movie King Kong, and always cry as if her heart would break when she watched Lassie.

⊷⊷◉⊶⊷

When Susie was eight, John's mom, Olive, had her second mastectomy. Susie heard about a bike-a-thon to raise money to fight cancer. She went around the neighborhood gathering pledges, then polished her bike and waited for the ride to begin.

We thought she would ride ten miles and raise "some" money, but Susie was the only child to end up finishing with the adults. She rode 50 miles, for grandmother. It was also when Susie was nine that John adopted her.

When Susie began fifth grade, we moved from Illinois to the Dallas-Fort Worth area. In just months, she acquired a Texas accent and embraced her new home and

friends. She became a member of the Texas Girl's Choir, and was later accepted at Camp Longhorn in her beloved "Texas hill country." I clearly remember driving down a country road one morning, a soft breeze caressing me, and being filled with such joy and peace, knowing life was very good.

⊷⊷◉⊶⊷

John later wrote: *Hardly a day passes that Susie's passion for living and her youthful wisdom are not vivid and bright in my thoughts and dreams. From little on, she was often the first one up in the morning but if I did need to wake her, I cannot recall a single time she did not open her eyes with a huge smile and want a wake up hug. She would begin at "speed," usually singing or hum-*

At Camp Longhorn, Burnet, Texas.

ming a tune and anxious to get going. If we had special plans for the day or a trip to take she would be out in front ready to soak in the new experience. Of course as the teenage years began the excitement remained but not necessarily focused around her parents!

When Susie entered Bedford Junior High, the principal and the counselor said Susie ranked very high on the IQ tests and qualified for special education. I told them I would never promote her to a higher grade or send her to a different school, that she loved her friends and being a kid.

I proudly marched home and told Susie the tests revealed that she was very smart, and asked her if she wanted to go to a special school that might challenge her more. Her answer was emphatically "NO," as I knew it would be.

"Since that is the case," I said, "I expect all A's in your school work."

"OK, Mom."

Hmmm. I thought that was too easy. However, she attended advanced classes, brought home top grades, and was fully involved and devoted to her school and schoolmates.

John wrote, *Susie was blessed with an acute awareness that life is about people and reaching out to others was as natural to her as breathing is to the rest of us. She loved to be around gaiety and positive people — negativity was not within Susie's character. If I were critical of something or someone she would argue the point or defend that person to the limit. It would upset me at times but I cannot help but admire her loyalty. If someone was hurting she was the first to help out with a kind word or a positive hug.*

There were times when Susie became so busy with her friends and schedule that I experienced pangs of sadness, and remembered when her world revolved much more around me. I remember thinking, "She was mine first, before her world became so much bigger."

I realized that my daughter was as great a friend to me as she was to the kids at school. I had had no close girlfriends until I was an adult, when I began to learn about friendship. My young years had isolated me as I focused on my mother's declining health. In many ways I was able to live another youth through Susie, for she enjoyed many of the activities I wished I had been able to do.

---◆◆◆---

In junior high school Susie gave her heart to gymnastics, and practiced with passionate dedication. She became team captain and loved her time spent in the gym with Coach Hightower and the kids on the team. Her friend, Tammy, would come by on her moped. Susie would hop on

the back, and off they went, with parents yelling at them to wear helmets. Susie, Rachel, Tammy, Debbie, Melissa, Leslie and her other friends developed a bond that kept growing.

At Bedford Junior High, she was Gymnastics Team Captain and made "Who's Who in Gymnastics." She served as V.P. of the Choir and was a Sweetheart nominee. She was voted Most Outstanding Student Council member, and belonged to the Pep Club and the National Junior Honor Society. She baby-sat for special families, knew how to clean and keep the house, bake a mean cookie and homemade bread. She began to have aspirations to go into medicine, like her Swope aunts and uncles.

Ken Moore, her beloved science teacher, wrote of "bringing her back to earth" and watching her grow and flourish with responsibilities, though "she had a science teacher who could have clubbed her several times."

One of my friends smiled and said, "Susie reminds me of a dancing sunbeam."

She kept up the pace at L.D. Bell High School. During her first year she was a member of the Regional Choir and Class Council and Student Council representative. In July of 1983 she studied at Oxford in England and NATO in Brussels as a delegate to the International Student Leadership Program Abroad. She returned home, appreciative of iced drinks, and became an avid reader and commentator on the news.

Bedford Jr. High School, 1982.

The teenage years had really "hit" when she was a junior in high school and we were grateful it had not come earlier. Susie was still making good grades and involved in all her activities, but she seemed ungrounded, agonizing about relationships, questioning and rebellious toward us.

An attorney friend of mine had introduced me to a gifted intuitive, who impressed with his integrity and his wisdom. I kept feeling that it would be good for Susie to see him. I made an appointment for her, asking her if she felt all right about this, and she tentatively agreed. At the appointment, I told him, "I'm trusting you with the prize of my life."

I had always taught Susie that the greatest gift we can give ourselves is to know ourselves. She had an hour session and left my friend's house smiling – with insights that led to greater peace in her whole being.

She told me then that he had described a specific (troublesome) friendship to her, and what it represented in her life. He described many of her friends in detail, their contributions in her life, and her contributions in theirs. He described her abilities in science, math and music, her personality, how she thrived on friends around her, her deep compassion for others and that she was a very powerful and wise soul.

Susie later told me, *Mom, he said I might be an astronaut when I'm older, that in the future he saw me studying in space or traveling among the stars.*

I will forever be grateful to my instincts, for trusting myself and letting Susie have that experience. It moved her to insights, to more understanding of her life and the world around her. After that first intuitive reading, she seemed stronger and more grounded. It was a strength she would build on in the coming years.

-·>═◉ ◉═<·-

During her high school years, John began "date nights" with her. Once a month, on a Friday night, he took her out. When she was a senior, a young man called and asked her for a date, and she said, "I'm sorry, I have a date with my Dad on Friday night." The young man couldn't believe it, but she said, "Yep, it's true." They went to movies, plays, car shows, festivals, and dinner, coming home happy and delighted; they both loved their special time together.

Susie went through a smoking phase, supposed to be unknown to us, but her dad was the first to know. She hid a pack of cigarettes in her glove compartment and he found them. He inserted a card beneath the cellophane, on which he wrote, "'Hi, Susie.' Dad.'

One day during her junior year, he asked her to go for a ride with him. He drove a couple of blocks, parked the car near some empty lots, pulled out a pack of cigarettes, and offered her one.

She replied, "Oh no, Dad, no thank you. I don't want to smoke."

He said, "Oh, sure you do, let's sit here and smoke," and pushed the pack at her.

She protested, "No, Dad, I really don't want to."

He lit one and gave it to her, "I know you like to smoke. Let's share a cigarette." He lit one for himself and her. Susie held hers, and refused to smoke in front of him.

Susie related this story to me a few times, each time laughing until the tears rolled from her eyes. She thought it was the worst and the funniest moment, that her Dad had backed her to the wall about smoking, she trying to maintain it, knowing that he knew, but not wanting to confess. She said, "I wanted to crawl out of that car door and disappear."

⤙⟞⊙⟨⤚

One Saturday night she came home with definite beer breath. Early the next morning, John went into her room and rousted her out of bed. He had her outside weeding the hill in front of the house, slapping at bugs, stabbing at the dirt. She had a headache, and sent us bad looks, her eyes smudged with mascara.

Years later, I heard her relate to other young people, "Do you know what MY parents did to me?" She sounded pleased and proud, as if she had a battle flag to take out and wave. She would say, "You think you've been grounded? No, no. We have to talk. I'll tell you what grounding is...."

She told me that a young man was pursuing her, wanting to be "with her," and he sometimes made crude remarks in the school hall to her. She had a lovely bosom, but hated it when guys referred to her "tops."

Her locker was down the hall from this boy's, and one day he yelled to her, something about "doing it with him."

Susie had reached the end of her patience with this guy. She shouted back, across the crowded hall, as she slammed her locker, "And lose it to you?"

She came home and told me she said this. I swallowed hard and said, "You did? You said that in a crowded hall?" Wow.

Susie with her three Swope aunts: Polly, Jane & Betsy 1982.

I had no experience with this kind of youthful conversation. Was this the norm? Did guys really talk like this, or young women answer so honestly and openly?

Until her junior year, I had been able to talk her out of growing up in a hurry. I would say, "That can wait for you, just enjoy what this time offers. You have your whole life to be an adult."

And she did occasionally listen to Mom's advice. Even the year before, I overheard her talking on the telephone to a girlfriend. "Hey, let's just be kids, we're going to have to be grown up soon enough."

I could have sunk to my knees with joy, for my headstrong daughter gave so few signs of hearing my words. I felt sometimes that I was talking to myself – or to the wind. I spent many evenings sitting on the foot of her bed, as we talked about anything and everything. I supported her, yet tried to put on the brakes.

Later, her friend Rachel wrote, "Sometimes it takes more strength to let kids do their own thing, when parents are needed, but appreciated to stay 'behind the scenes.' Your home was there for us, and you and John were two of the few parents chosen to be included in our high school lives. Thank you for those memories."

Every Friday afternoon after school the house was full of kids painting signs in the garage and driveway for the football games. I remember cooking large quantities of food and the kids running in and out of the house, laughing and full of life. I loved those days.

A friend wrote, "My memories jump to this vivacious, beautiful young woman in Texas, being involved in everything, besides working, too! And I remember her having this brick-house type body that no teenager should be so blessed with…"

In Susie's senior year she was V.P. of the Explorer Group at HEB Harris Hospital, a Student Council Representative, a member of Class Council, Young Life, F.C.A., and National Honor Society. No wonder our heads were spinning.

Susie and Robert Van Til. 1985.

A counselor at Bell High School wrote, "In writing this letter of recommendation I find it difficult to find a place to start with this young lady. Susie Swope is one of the most energetic, inspiring, dedicated, and mature students that I have come in contact with in a long time. We recently served as the host school for approximately 800 Student Council representatives from the southern states. Here Susie showed her real leadership abilities. She was the 'take charge' person in the organization and implementation of the conference. You can look at her transcript and it will reveal her academic success, but it will not indicate her involvement with her school and community."

Susie and Rachel. Graduation 1985.

→⇥═◉═⇤←

Years later, Kristie Fox, wrote, "Susie was full of such energy and always made any situation O.K. I think that is what I liked the most about her. She always made you feel like what was going on in your life, although bad, would turn out good. If I could choose a friend to go through life with, it would be her."

Kathy, wrote, *"Dear Northwest Mom, for the past seven years now my thoughts are especially intense about Susie during March. I was driving to work the other day and the Chicago song, "A Hard Habit To Break," came over the radio.*

"In high school, we all used to gather at your house and make signs for the pep rally and game on Friday. We got paint all over your driveway and permanent marker on our

clothes, and continually romped through your house while you fed us. In addition, we cranked the radio up as loud as we could. Those were great times. One of my favorite recollections of these gatherings is an impromptu lip sync performance given by Susie and Anne Marie to the above song. I still crack up thinking of their performance. They were such the drama queens! The memory still makes me smile. I thought I'd share it with you so we could smile together. All my love, Kath."

In talking to Rachel one evening, I told her I sometimes did not know what the writing was all about. It became an act of faith that I would pick up and lay down. She said, *Well, I know. It's the very essence of life. It's learning about*

Susie. Summer of 1987.

the higher plane while you're in an earthbound existence. I thanked Susie for the presence and wisdom of her friends.

John wrote, *Being Susie's Dad has been the most rewarding period of my life. It was by no means a role of simply showing up and proceeding with the basic responsibilities of providing, protecting and loving. From the very beginning it was apparent that our journey together was going to require my total involvement, commitment, honesty, sharing and unconditional love.*

Living with Susie brought with it the realization that all human emotions are to be experienced and living life passionately is a basic requirement of being here. It was a personal awakening for me and an experience unlike any other that has given my life purpose, enrichment and fulfillment. She is missed beyond words.

TWO FRIENDS ~ A TRIBUTE

It is almost certain that between friends there is at all times a silent communication, a sort of unconscious mental conversation, going on.
The Science of Mind

Our lives are filled with the echoes of time; the imprint of voices and memory float through and we remember so clearly family, friends and moments that have touched our hearts. I give thanks for all those people and experiences that have been loving friends and teachers. Reine Hillis and Jerri Davis will always be regarded as gifts in my life. Their friendship, love and acceptance simply blessed me. I grieved when both women were diagnosed with cancer, believing they would heal, but this was not to be. During Reine's last week she was aware but could speak very little. A few days before she passed on, I felt her with me and that she wanted me to write to her children. I sat down and told her, "I am here for you." The following words flowed through me and are universal in their mother love. I dedicate them to Reine and Jerri, two beautiful friends who taught me much about the warmth and healing power of love.

I will miss you. I love you very much and am so grateful you are my children. I am overwhelmingly proud of you. Memories and pictures float in and out of time, the smallest moment held for me to re-experience.

I remember every baby curve of your bodies, every adolescent change, the joy of being surrounded by you as adults and having you as my friends as well as children. I will miss our time together, all of it. The hard times, the celebrations, the learning, the laughter, simply being together. You have assisted my growth and helped me become what I aspired to be. All the places and moments we shared; they are a wealth of memories I want you to hold with joy and pleasure.

This illness has often been overwhelming and bewildered my body and mind, and I fought to stay here with all my resources. I believe in healing, but am being called elsewhere, being brought to another place I call home. I am aware of being between two worlds and of feeling an expansive, beautiful, loving universe. I am being held in the most loving of hands.

You have given me immense joy and that is what fills me now, spills over and around me. Please know this…my body is what you are seeing, but change and new beginnings are often hard. You know my spirit and my beliefs. Please, remember them now and see beyond what you are seeing. We are all so much more than our bodies and this moment. Know this and bring your awareness to this knowledge.

In this room, I feel your presence and have looked into your eyes and am filled with deep sadness that partings have to hurt so much. I never wanted you to have this pain. I would do anything to take your hurt away, but I cannot. Let the pain heal…it is not for you to keep. And know that I am your Mother who loves you completely always. You will feel me. You will know me.

ABOUT THE AUTHOR

Mollie M. Swope is the mother of a young woman who, after death, communicated with her in spirit and dream form to reveal insights into life and death. Author of several published articles, she does grief counseling and works with young adults with major illnesses, and is presently working on another book. A graduate of the University of Washington, she worked for years as a real estate broker and presently owns and manages a guest house on Whidbey Island, Washington. She and her husband John, reside in Bellevue, Washington.

TO ORDER THIS BOOK

Please send $16.00
(includes postage and handling) to

MOLLIE M. SWOPE
P.O. BOX 52925
BELLEVUE, WA 98015-2925

or order through her website: LegacyPress.net

You are invited to share your thoughts
and/or your own experiences with the author
and others through LegacyPress.net

READING
without Books

Julie Burns
Dorothy Swan

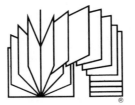

A FEARON MAKEMASTER® BOOK

Fearon Pitman Publishers, Inc.
Belmont, California

Design by Paul Quin
Art by Julie Burns
Cover design by Wayne and Linda Bonnett

ISBN-0-8224-5830-6

Printed in the United States of America.

1. 9 8 7 6 5 4 3 2 1

CONTENTS

INTRODUCTION

"How can we improve our reading instruction? This question may be among those most frequently asked by parents, teachers, administrators, and even politicians. Research indicates that a strong developmental program, using a basal reader with additional phonics, is successful in teaching most children to read. Equally important, but difficult to achieve, are the tasks of making reading relevant to individual students and motivating the students to apply their reading skills. Enrichment of the basal approach is essential to create a complete, comprehensive reading program.

Teachers have a great opportunity to take advantage of the wide vocabulary exposure, practical experience, and natural motivating qualities of the actual items, other than books, which students are reading in their daily lives: magazines, labels, advertisements, TV guides, telephone books, and so on. The students' confidence in handling these materials, and the frequency of their use, can be greatly enhanced by classroom instruction—with a concomitant increase in reading skills and knowledge of the importance of reading.

Reading without Books is a supplementary reading program that can be individualized to meet the abilities and interests of your own class. It takes advantage of the known usefulness and superiority of teacher-made materials in contrast to preprogrammed kits which may not precisely meet your needs.

Students will participate in the program by collecting many of the materials themselves; thus they are involved in providing what is to be read and not merely in reading material gathered by the teacher. This kind of participation can build in the student's mind a bridge between the "reading class" at school and the objects and words which are a natural part of his or her everyday life.

This book provides reading activities in categories other than fiction or nonfiction books. Each section includes teaching suggestions designed for elementary students in the form of large and small group activities, worksheets, or task cards—many of which are also appropriate for junior-high use. Every effort has been made to make these ideas as flexible and adaptable to the individual classroom situation as possible. The MAKEMASTER® worksheets are designed to be removed so that multiple copies can be made. The reproduced task cards can be cut apart and mounted on tagboard so that individual students or partners may choose a card and complete the assigned task. Perhaps you would prefer to duplicate a page for the entire class so they can complete it as part of a weekly contract. Add to the collection of task cards as you and your students come up with new ideas.

The ideas in this book offer only a few of the ways that materials used frequently by the students can be incorporated into your reading program. Be creative! Let these ideas be a springboard to the discovery of many more materials in our environment which can add variety, enrichment, and interest to your reading program.

THE SHOPPING TOWER

Obtain the Materials

The Shopping Tower can be made out of a tall crate or two or more cardboard boxes stacked on top of one another and taped together. The children are instructed to bring from home labels to be glued to the tower. They may bring any type—the fronts of boxes of soap, toothpaste, cake mixes, cereals, and milk cartons; they may cut out the fronts of sacks of flour, bread, sugar, and dog food; they may remove the paper labels from cans, bottles, and meats. When the students paste the labels to the tower, they should overlap them slightly to create a wallpaper effect. Remind them to cut the labels out carefully, although all need not be the same shape or symmetrical. For added incentive divide the children into four teams and assign each team one side of the tower. Let the teams have a contest to see which can cover its side first.

Begin Your Study by Discussing

Use the following questions in leading a class discussion. The area of concern for each question is included in italics.

- What is your favorite product on the tower?   *Skimming*

- Which product has the prettiest pictures or the most attractive labels? Would you be more likely to buy this product at the store? Will it taste best?   *Consumer education*

- If you had all these products, which ones would you choose to make a well-rounded meal?   *Health*

- What product weighs the most? the least? Check the weights. Does the heaviest product come in the largest container?   *Consumer education*

- Do you see any meat labels? Why aren't there more?   *Reasoning*

- What product might cost the most? Are any prices listed? Compare prices.   *Math*

- Can you find any two things that go together like eggs and bacon or bread and butter?   *Analogous relationships*

- How many brands can you find of the same product?   *Skimming*

- Have you seen ads for any of these things on TV? Would you be more likely to buy things you've seen advertised?   *Consumer education*

Practicing with the Shopping Tower

- Brand Names. *Have the students find as many brand names as they can that start with the letters T or B. (Adapt this exercise to whatever you are studying in class: blends, vowels, synonyms, syllables, compound words, or the like.)*

- Categories. *Make categories. Allow the children to list all the fruits, vegetables, desserts, things that are not food, things that are bought in cans, things that probably cost over one dollar, or all the products put out by a certain company.*

- Prices. *Have the students list anything they can find that has the price on it. (They may list the items individually and then add the prices together.)*

- Favorite Products. *For homework, have your students write down their five favorite products from the tower. Have them take their lists to the grocery store when they go with their families and find out how much each product costs.*

Name_____

THE SHOPPING TOWER

Directions : You will need to look at a shopping
tower to do this worksheet.

1. What is your favorite food on the tower?

   _____

2. Find two labels for mixes (pudding, cake, and the like).

   _____   _____

3. Make up a dinner using only items you find on the tower.

   Meat or Cheese _____

   Vegetable _____

   Fruit _____

   Bread _____

   Dessert _____

   Beverage _____

4. On the tower, find two different labels which advertise the
   same kind of product. Write the name of the product
   and also the two brand names.

   <u>Product</u> _____   <u>Brand</u> _____

                                                         <u>Brand</u> _____

5. Find four compound words on the tower.

   _____   _____

   _____   _____

6. Turn this paper over and make a label of your own for a
   real or pretend product. Be sure to include the brand
   name, list of contents, weight, price, and picture.

USING
CEREAL
BOXES

Obtain the Materials

Cereal boxes should be easy to collect. Ask each student to bring in an empty box. You may want to gather a set in which every box is different for task card use.

Begin Your Study by Discussing

Discuss the information that can be found on a cereal box, including:

- Name
- Chief grain and other ingredients
- Company
- Weight
- Price
- Things that are free or can be sent for
- Nutritional breakdown
- Computer code for price and ease of purchase
- Recipes
- Slogans

Practicing with Cereal Boxes

☐ Write a Letter. *Have the children send for some item that is being offered on a cereal package. Use the following outline to instruct them in the proper form.*

Date
Your street address
Your city, state, and zip

Name of company you're writing to
Its street address
Its city, state, and zip

Dear Cereal Maker:

(Write your own words here)

Sincerely,

Your name

☐ Plan an Advertising Campaign. *Discuss different ways breakfast cereal companies encourage consumers to buy their products. Include TV ads, free offers, money-off coupons, health and energy emphasis, attractive packaging, and so on. Now let the students plan their own advertising campaign for "Crunchy Wunchies" or a cereal with an original name of their choice. They should include:*

☐ *Box design*
☐ *Slogan or song*
☐ *Free toys*
☐ *Billboards*
☐ *Ingredients*
☐ *Price*
☐ *Recipes using the product*
☐ *Testimonials by famous people*

Name _____

WHAT'S ON A CEREAL BOX?

Directions: You will need an empty cereal
   box to do this worksheet. All the
   answers will be found on your cereal box.

1. The name of your cereal is _____

2. What company makes your cereal? _____

   Where is it located? _____

3. The package weighs _____

4. If you had some of your cereal in your hand, describe
   what it would look like. _____

   _____

5. How much did your cereal cost? _____

6. List four ingredients found in your cereal.

   _____   _____

   _____   _____

7. Write about one of the following from your box: 1) Copy
   a recipe found on your box. 2) Describe the "send-away"
   offer. 3) Explain what the "surprise" in the box probably
   looked like. 4) Tell something you learned from reading the box.

   _____

   _____

   _____

   _____

8. On the back of this paper, design your own cereal
   box. Be sure to include the weight, ingredients,
   a free offer or surprise, and a colorful box.

Look at the name of a cereal. Can you use those letters to make some new words? Can you make six new words? ten new words?

Jack
Crunchos
so
run
sum

Name at least seven vitamins. You will find them listed on the side of the cereal boxes. List the vitamins in alphabetical order.

Write the weights of the cereal in four different boxes. For each cereal write its name and weight. Underline the cereal that is the heaviest.

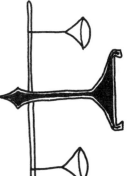

Look on four cereal boxes. Write the name of the cereal and its expiration date. (Some boxes will not have a date, so look through all the boxes until you find four that do.)

MARCH
	1	2	3	4
5	6	7	8	9	10	11
12	13	14	15	16	17	18
19	20	21	22	23	24	25
26	27	28	29	30	31	

Look on one of the cereal boxes to find out what percentage of the cereal is fat. What percentage is protein? How many calories are there in an average serving?

Peter

1-syllable words	2-syllable words	3-syllable words
fat	protein	vitamin

Divide your paper into these three columns

Good Work

Look on the cereal boxes for ten words in each column. Write them on your paper.

Look for a cereal box that has a recipe on it. Copy the recipe. If you made it at home, how do you think it would taste?

COOKIES

We were made from Zippo cereal.

Find some cereal boxes that have "free offers" or things to send away for. Write down the name of three cereals and the offer for each one. For each offer write down what you have to send (one boxtop and 50¢).

FROM Zippo

Invent a new cereal. Include these facts:

1) The name of your cereal.
2) How your cereal looks and tastes.
3) A recipe or free offer to send for.
4) Draw a box front.

List the names of six different cereals and the company that makes each one.

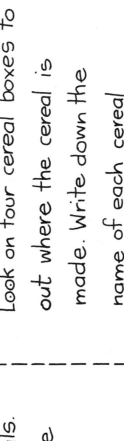

Look for the price of four cereals. (Some boxes may not have the price on them.) Write the name of each cereal and its price on your paper. Underline the most expensive cereal.

Look on four cereal boxes to find out where the cereal is made. Write down the name of each cereal and the location of the plant where it is made.

9

Make up a story about an animal or person from one of the cereal boxes.

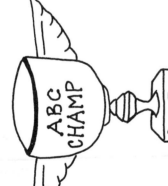

Write down the names of ten of the cereals your class has collected. Put the names in alphabetical order. Circle your favorite cereal.

ABC CHAMP

GOOD JOB

Pretend that some Martians just landed in your backyard. Their first question is, "What is cereal?" What would you tell them?

Then what would you do?

USA

Write a script for a commercial about your very favorite cereal.

SUPER TV

Announcer: "Wow! Everyone loves Quackoa, our favorite cereal!"

Sound Effects: "Quack! Quack!"

CHECK THE TELEPHONE BOOK

Obtain the Materials

The time to collect telephone books is right after the new ones have come out. Students will be happy to bring in their old books, and many businesses with multiple phones (and books) could supply you with an ample number.

Begin Your Study by Discussing

☐ The Telephone Book

1. Discuss the importance of the emergency numbers inside the front cover.

2. Examine the index. Be sure the children know the meaning of collect calls, long-distance rates, mobile and marine service, prefixes, and so on. Refer to the page on definitions.

3. Discuss prefix locations and variations in rates for different days and times.

4. Discuss the difference between white and yellow pages.

5. Discuss the guide words at the top of each page.

☐ A Classroom Directory

1. Give each child a telephone book.

2. List on the board all the names of children in the class whose family or home number is in the book.

3. After each child's name put in parentheses the name under which the phone number is listed, but not the number.

4. Have the students copy the names and then look up their classmates' numbers for the directory.

5. Students may keep this directory for their own use.

Practice with the Telephone Book

☐ "Stand-Up" Quiz Game for Alphabetizing

1. Write a name and address from the telephone book on the blackboard.

2. Have the children look for the telephone number of this person. As they find it, they stand up.

3. After about half the class has found the number and is standing, call on the first pupil who stood up. If that child gives the correct number, he or she gets a bean or a paper token. If he or she is wrong, the second child who stood gets an opportunity to answer. A correct answer is again rewarded with a token.

4. Write another name on the board, and repeat the procedure. Continue for several rounds.

5. The winner is the child with the most beans or paper tokens.

6. For a variation, choose businesses from the yellow pages for the students to look up.

☐ "Thumbs Left, Thumbs Right" Guide-Word Game

1. The children open their telephone books to the same page.

2. Pick a name from one of the two exposed pages and say it aloud.

3. By looking at the guide words at the top of the page, the students decide if the name is on the left page or the right page. They point with their thumbs in the direction which indicates which page it is on.

4. After locating several names on the open pages, flip to a new section of the telephone book. Repeat the procedure.

☐ Long-Distance Math Lesson

▫ After studying the rates for local and nearby dialing areas, let the students find out what the cost would be for three calls to (city of your choice), one call to (another city of your choice), and two calls to (a third city of your choice). Repeat, by using any combination of calls at your children's ability level.

▫ For more advanced students use the prefixes and overtime rates on the next pages.

▫ For good practice in reading graphs, make up problems using the long-distance rates for various locations and at different times of the day and week.

☐ Phone Challengers. *The following questions might be used as a basis for class discussions. Students might also be divided into smaller groups to search out their own answers. Questions like these are good for vocabulary building, categorizing, alphabetizing, and solving practical problems students might meet in real-life situations.*

☐ You've just moved into a new neighborhood, and you don't have a car. You must find a doctor, lawyer, and a church to attend that are close to your home.   *Hint for the teacher: Look in the yellow pages for "Physicians," "Attorneys," and "Churches."*

☐ You want to call the theater to see what time the show starts. You cannot think of the name of the theater, but you would recognize it if you saw it.   *Hint: Use yellow pages.*

☐ Where can you buy a heavy-duty-equipment inner tube (bigger than a truck tire tube) to take to the lake on vacation?   *Hint: Look under "Tires" in the yellow pages. Try to find heavy-duty-equipment tires.*

☐ What is the number of the main branch of the city library? You want to know if they have a special book.   *Hint: Look for "City Offices," under the name of the city.*

☐ Where can you apply for a job selling newspapers? What number would you call?   *Hint: Call the newspaper office.*

☐ Who can you call to find out the nearest place to get a work permit?   *Hint: Call the local high school.*

☐ You went to the beach with your family. The keys were accidentally locked in the trunk of the car. You have only one set of keys for the car. How do you get help? What kind of help?   *Hint: Call a locksmith.*

☐ Your poodle needs to be groomed and clipped. Where can you take it? Should you call for an appointment?   *Hint: Look under "Dog and Cat Grooming" in the yellow pages.*

☐ Where can you take judo lessons? What location is closest to home?   *Hint: Look under "Judo" in the yellow pages.*

☐ Where can you hire a "private eye"? How can you find out who would be best and what his or her fees would be? Write down the name and number of the one you choose and tell why you chose him or her.   *Hint: Look in the yellow pages for "Detectives" or "Investigators."*

☐ You're getting a doughboy pool in your back yard. You want to do most of the work yourself, but would like some help digging the hole. Who can help you?   *Hint: Look under "Excavating" in the yellow pages.*

☐ Your family wants to fly to Disneyland over Easter vacation. What company will you fly with? What questions will you ask the airlines?   *Hint: Ask questions about schedules, cost, meals, stopovers.*

☐ Is there someplace to call to get the weather report?   *Hint: Look in the yellow pages for "Weather Forecast Service."*

WHAT'S IN THE TELEPHONE BOOK?

Directions: You will need a telephone book to do this worksheet. Use the yellow pages.

1. Your mother needs some special medicine, and it is 2:00 A.M. Where could you go to get it?

   _____

2. You'd like to buy a motorcycle. Which shop will you go to first? Why? What makes of motorcycles do they carry?

   _____

   _____

3. Your family wants to go out to dinner. Choose a restaurant and write down its name and location.

   _____

4. Where could you buy a bicycle built for two? List two places.

   _____

   _____

5. You'd like to have some food delivered for your dinner. Where should you call, and what will you order?

   _____

6. You've sprained your ankle and must use crutches for several weeks. Where would you call to rent some crutches? List two places.

   _____

   _____

WHAT'S COOKING ?

Obtain the Materials

Recipes are abundant, and many children become very enthusiastic about making their own very favorite gourmet concoctions. In choosing a recipe for classroom preparation the very first consideration should be the suitability in the mode of preparation and cooking. Are the ingredients reasonably priced? Can the food be prepared in the classroom? Do you have the equipment to cook it conveniently?

Another important question you should ask is, "Can the cooking be done safely?" Keep the use of knives and hot oil to a minimum. Check your school-district policies about using electric appliances. Usually parent volunteers are happy to help supervise a group cooking activity and to see that safety regulations are being followed.

The recipes on the following pages have been chosen for their simplicity, ease of preparation, and taste appeal. You may copy the recipe on the board or duplicate the recipe for individual student copies.

Begin Your Study by Discussing

- ☐ What is your favorite food that is prepared in your house?
- ☐ What kinds of food can you prepare?
- ☐ What foods that have their origin in other countries do you like to eat? Do you know how to prepare them?
- ☐ What are some potential dangers in the kitchen? What precautions can be taken?
- ☐ What do the terms *baste, broil, pare, toss, blend, garnish, dice,* and others mean? *After choosing a recipe always make sure the children know the meanings of all special terms. Suggest that they use the dictionary if necessary.*

Practice with Recipes

☐ **Measuring Ingredients.** *Teach the importance of accurate measuring, and have a parent volunteer or capable child demonstrate how to sift and measure flour, how to pack brown sugar, how to accurately measure liquids, and how to pack and measure shortening.*

☐ **Converting Measurements.** *Spend some time studying a table of weights and measures. Give the children the opportunity to convert some of the measurements to other terms. Challenge them by letting them cut the ingredients for a recipe in half, or double or triple the quantities.*

☐ **Planning to Cook.** *Usually the children, working in small groups, will plan their own cooking experiences. To help develop their social skills and a sense of responsibility, allow them to figure out what ingredients and utensils are needed and who will bring each item.*

☐ **Looking at Recipes.** *Discuss the various parts of a recipe.*

    ☐ *The name of the dish (What is it called?)*

    ☐ *The ingredients (What do you need to make it?)*

    ☐ *The procedure (What do you do—mix, chop, and so on?)*

    ☐ *Cooking time and temperature (How hot should the oven or stove be, and how long should the food be cooked?)*

    ☐ *Serving method (How do you arrange the food on the plate?)*

    ☐ *Number of servings (How many can eat what you have cooked?)*

☐ **Making a Class Recipe Book.** *Ask each student to bring in his or her favorite recipe from home. If you want accurate and correct recipes, parents should be involved, and you may use the letter on page 17 for each child to take home. Or if you are planning to give the recipe collection as a gift to the parents (for Christmas, Mother's Day, or Father's Day), students can either dictate or write down their recollection of their favorite recipes. An excellent book, Smashed Potatoes by Jane Martel ($2.95, New York: Houghton-Mifflin, 1973) provides a collection of delightful recipes by young children.*

    Write the recipes on dittos, and have students collate the pages so that each child can have a copy of the class recipe book. Each student can design his or her own cover.

Dear _____ :

    We are working on a class recipe book at school. Each of us is going to bring in a favorite recipe. Then the recipes will be dittoed and we will get copies to assemble into our own books.

    Could you please help me copy down a recipe for _____? I'll need to include these things:

1. Ingredients
2. Preparation procedure
3. Cooking time and temperature
4. Serving method
5. Number of servings

I should return my recipe by _____.

    Thank you for your help.

              Love,

             _____

ROASTED PUMPKIN SEEDS

1⅓ cup pumpkin seeds
1⅓ cup water
3 tablespoons salt

Wash all the yellow fibers off the pumpkin seeds.
Spread the seeds on paper towels, and let them
dry for 72 hours. Bring the water and salt
to a boil, stirring once or twice. Pour this
mixture over the pumpkin seeds. Cover
and leave for 24 hours.
Pour off the water, and spread seeds on a
cookie sheet. Place in a 350°F oven for
about half an hour or until the seeds
are dry and puffed up. Cool, and then eat!

LITTLE PIZZAS

2 29=ounce jars of meatless
   spaghetti sauce
1 8=ounce package shredded
   mozzarella cheese
¼ cup shredded Parmesan cheese
2 teaspoons oregano leaves
1 teaspoon instant chopped onion
¼ teaspoon garlic salt
1 loaf sliced french bread.

Mix the first six ingredients together. Spread this pizza
mixture on slices of french bread. Toast in a toaster
oven until top is bubbly.

[Serves 15]

18

APPLESAUCE WITH RED HOTS

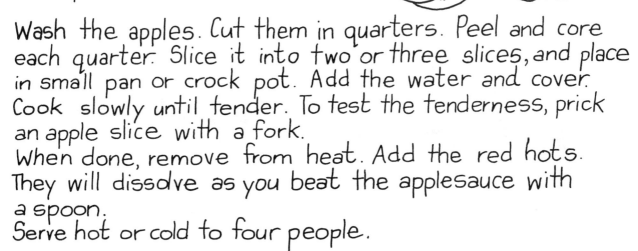

4 apples (green ones are best)

¼ cup water

¼ cup red hot candies

Wash the apples. Cut them in quarters. Peel and core each quarter. Slice it into two or three slices, and place in small pan or crock pot. Add the water and cover. Cook slowly until tender. To test the tenderness, prick an apple slice with a fork.

When done, remove from heat. Add the red hots. They will dissolve as you beat the applesauce with a spoon.

Serve hot or cold to four people.

- -

UNBAKED CHOCOLATE COOKIES

½ cup milk

½ cube butter or margarine

2 cups sugar

6 tablespoons cocoa

3½ cups instant oatmeal

1 cup chopped nuts

Boil the milk, margarine, sugar, and cocoa in a pan for three minutes, stirring continuously. Add the oatmeal and nuts to the mixture in the pan. Mix well.

Wash your hands well. Shape dough into balls the size of a walnut, and place on waxed paper to cool and harden.

[Makes about three dozen cookies]

MAKE-YOUR-OWN ICE CREAM

Metal Juice Can

COTTAGE CHEESE CARTON

Your Own Ice Cream Freezer

1 quart half-and-half
¾ quart milk
1 can sweetened condensed milk
2 small packages instant pudding (any flavor)
crushed ice and salt

Mix liquids and pudding together. Pour into regular ice cream freezer, or pour into 10 metal juice cans. Put cans in 10 cottage cheese cartons. Put crushed ice and about one tablespoon salt around the juice can. Stir ice cream with a spoon until slushy.   Serves 10

HINT To make crushed ice, freeze water in empty milk cartons. Pound carton with hammer, open carton, and remove crushed ice!

[Serves 10]

- -

FRYING PAN BISCUITS

2 cups flour
3¾ teaspoons baking powder
1 teaspoon salt
⅓ cup cooking oil
¾ cup milk
butter and jam

Sift together flour, baking powder, and salt. Stir in oil and milk. Using just a little flour, roll out dough ¼ inch thick. Using a blunt knife or cookie cutters, cut dough into shapes. Cook in lightly greased electric fry pan set at low heat. Let biscuits brown and rise. Turn and cook other side-about 10 minutes total. Serve with butter and jam.

Berry Jam

CHEESE PRETZELS

¼ teaspoon yeast
3 tablespoons warm water
½ teaspoon sugar
½ cup flour
2 tablespoons grated cheese
1 egg
1 tablespoon coarse salt

Dissolve yeast in warm water. Add sugar, flour, and cheese. Blend until dough is smooth. Knead dough. When well mixed, divide into four pieces. Roll dough into ropes and form into pretzel shapes or other fun shapes. Brush with beaten egg; sprinkle with salt. Bake in 425°F. oven for 15 minutes until brown.

[Makes four pretzels]

PIGS-IN-BLANKETS

2 cups purchased biscuit mix
1 package hot dogs
½ cup cold water

Make dough by mixing biscuit mix and water. Knead dough and then roll it out. Cut the dough into squares. Wrap squares of dough around one-fourth or one-half of a hot dog.
Place on greased baking sheet, and bake at 450°F. for 10-12 minutes or until brown.

MAGAZINES PLUS !

Obtain the Materials

Magazines are usually available in abundance. Students can often bring them from home. Children's magazines are especially good for classroom work. Different issues of the same magazine make the basis for effective learning centers. Flea markets, garage sales, and discards from the library are also good sources. Sometimes a retail store that has unsold, old magazines is able to give them to you for classroom work. You might also solicit magazine distributors for free copies.

Begin Your Study by Discussing

☐   Kinds of Magazines. For what kind of reader was the magazine written? Why would a person be interested in this kind of magazine? Ask the same question about other magazines, and compare the answers.

☐   Different Parts of the Magazine. If possible, all the children should have different issues of the same magazine. After browsing through the magazine they should be able to identify the cover page, issue and date, table of contents, ads, and special features. Write the different parts on the blackboard. Make the list as complete as possible.

Practice with Magazines

What's in a Magazine?

☐ Have the children look through a magazine and find the place where it tells how to subscribe, then fill out the subscription form. How much does a subscription for one year cost? for two years? How much would they save with a two-year subscription?

☐ Have the children examine the table of contents and write down the titles and page numbers of three stories or articles that interest them.

☐ Have the children find an ad for something they like and write down the name of the item. Ask them to tell what it looks like or what it does and how much it costs.

Creative Writing Activities

☐ Ask each child to read a story and make a comic strip about it. Have them draw several pictures of things that happen and use balloons to show what people or animals are saying.

☐ Have each child cut out a picture from the magazine and make up a story about the picture, then paste the picture on a paper and write the story under it. Remind the children to give their stories titles.

☐ Have each child write a different ending for a story he or she has read in the magazine and draw two pictures. One picture should show how the original story ended, and one should illustrate the child's version of the ending.

☐ Have each child make an advertisement for some story or article he or she has read in the magazine. Have each child draw a picture of something he or she found interesting in the story and write a sentence about it that will make others want to read it. Remind the children to write the title of the story and author as well as the name and date of the magazine, so that others can find it to read.

Words and More Words

☐ *Ask each child to make a picture dictionary by making a booklet out of newsprint and putting a letter of the alphabet on each page in alphabetical order. Have them try to find pictures with the same beginning sound as the letter on the page, then cut out the pictures and paste them on the appropriate pages. If they cannot find a picture to illustrate a specific letter, they may draw a picture. It might be fun to work in committees or pairs for this activity.*

☐ *Ask each child to read a story and choose ten interesting words from the story, then write each word and draw a picture of it.*

☐ *Ask each child to read a story and look for five words with one syllable, five two-syllable words, and five three-syllable words, then write them down. Can they find a word with four syllables? five?*

☐ *Have each child look for eight words with long-vowel sounds and eight words with short-vowel sounds and write them down and mark the vowel sounds. Can they find any words that have a short- and a long-vowel sound?*

☐ *Have each child read a story and list ten action words. Action words are run, laugh, hop, and the like. Have the children make up sentences using two or more of their words and draw a picture for the sentence.*

☐ *Have each child read a story and find words beginning with the same letter as his or her first name. If a child finds fewer than ten words, ask him or her to look for words beginning with the first letter of the last name.*

☐ *Ask each child to read a story and look for compound words. If the child cannot find them in the story, ask him or her to think of some. Ask the children to change the last word or the first word of each compound to make up a new compound word.*

Write a letter to the editor telling him or her why you like the magazine and suggest some improvements or future articles.

"How about an article on owls, especially what they like to eat?"

Look through your magazine to find an advertisement for something you'd like to buy. Tell why you want it.

Look through your magazine to find a joke section. Write down a joke that you find and also another joke that you know.

LET'S LAUGH!

Name four things found in your magazine that are not stories. List them.

READ MORE!
BE SMART!!

Pretend you are a writer and must write a review of a story for a newspaper. What is your opinion of the story? What are its strengths and weaknesses? Would you recommend it to your friends?

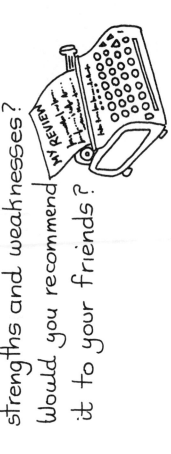

Read a story and write down ten words that are <u>verbs</u>. Verbs are action words like run, jump, or laugh. Next to each verb, put another form of the verb that you know.

slam

run-runs

see-saw

hop-hopped

List the following facts from your story:

Who :

What:

When:

Where:

Why :

Choose a character from your story and tell how you would spend the day together. Tell where you would go. What games would you play? What would you talk about, and what would you eat for your lunch?

Read a story and look for words with prefixes and suffixes. Write down five words with prefixes and five words with suffixes. For each word, try to think of another word that has the same prefix or suffix.

remake

replaying   jumping

prefix   suffix

Find some sentences in a story with adjectives and adverbs. Rewrite those sentences using _different_ adjectives and adverbs. They do not have to mean the same as those in the story.

hungry
The _sloppy_ giant was very _grouchy_.

pretty

Read a story from your magazine and list eight descriptive words. Descriptive words tell about something — fast, pretty, tall. Use three or more of your words to describe something.

This clown certainly is funny, tall, and clever.

Write a new episode of a story you have read using the same characters. You could have the story take place at a different time or location.

LOOK for this STORY   NEW TIME   NEW PLACE

Look through your story for contractions. Write down six contractions and the two words that make up each contraction.

isn't = is not

Your story has just been selected as one of the new TV shows for next season. The producer wants outlines of the first three shows. Write a few sentences about what would happen in each show.

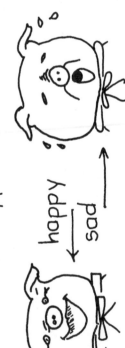

Rewrite the ending of your story. You may want to add a new character or have something unusual happen.

Look through your story for some words that have opposites. Write down ten words and their opposites.

happy
←→
sad

WHAT'S ON A MENU?

Obtain the Materials

Menus can be the source of many interesting lessons. Chain restaurants often use menus as place mats and are very generous about giving them to teachers for classroom use. Newspaper-style menus are frequently used by ice cream parlors and are easily obtainable. Pizza parlors often have take-home price lists that could be obtained in classroom quantities. A child might like to copy McDonald's price list on a poster so that the class can compare it with another child's price list from another local short-order restaurant. A duplicating master can be made from a menu so that each class member will have his or her own copy.

Begin Your Study by Discussing

- ☐ Terms like a la mode, a la carte, and entree
- ☐ Different sections of the menu
- ☐ Different kinds of food unfamiliar to the pupils
- ☐ Tipping (who gets the tip, why it's given, how much)
- ☐ Restaurant manners
- ☐ A good order for an afternoon snack
- ☐ A good order for breakfast or dinner

Practicing with Menus

☐ The Waiter and Waitress Game (Developing Auditory Memory). *Divide the children into groups of four or five. Let one child be the waiter or waitress. The others in the group, who are customers, give the waiter or waitress their orders. The first time, they order just a beverage or dessert from the menu. The waiter or waitress pretends to leave the room; then he or she comes back and says the name of each imaginary dish being set before the customers. The children take turns being a waiter or waitress. As their facility increases, they may order complete meals with choice of salad dressing and dessert.*

☐ Math Activities

    ☐ Order a meal. Draw a picture of it. Write the price, and tell what the tip should be.

    ☐ If you had only $.50, what things on the menu could you buy?

    ☐ What is the most expensive thing on the menu?

    ☐ What could you buy two friends and yourself at the restaurant if you had only $3.00?

    ☐ How much would a full meal for your whole family cost? Include beverages and tip. Tell what you ordered for each person.

    ☐ If the whole family got a meal at McDonald's, how much would it cost? Tell what you ordered for each one in the family. Compare this price with the answer for the question above. What is the difference?

☐ Reading and Language Activities

    ☐ Underline all the adjectives in the menu. Circle the best-sounding food.

    ☐ Find as many compound words as you can.

    ☐ Find four words that are new to you. Look them up in the dictionary, and write the meaning on paper.

    ☐ Write six singular nouns with their plural forms (either of which can be on the menu).

    ☐ Find as many prefixes and suffixes as you can. Underline the prefixes in red and the suffixes in green.

☐ Creative Writing Activities

    ☐ Write an entry for some favorite food you'd like to add to the menu. Name it, describe it, and include the price.

    ☐ Start your own restaurant. Pick out an original name, decide what kinds of food you want to serve, and make up your own menu. Describe each food, and include the price.

Name _____

WHAT'S ON A MENU?

Sam's Sandwich Shop

Directions: You will need a menu to do this work-sheet. All the answers will be found on your menu.

1. The name of your restaurant is _____

2. What is your favorite thing on this menu?

   _____

3. Using your menu, order an entire meal. Choose a

   sandwich _____

   beverage _____

   dessert _____

4. What is the most expensive item on your menu? List the item and its cost.

   _____   _____

5. Menus use descriptive words to tell about their food. Find five descriptive words such as "fresh", "tasty", or "delicious". List them.

   _____   _____

   _____   _____

6. Write any five items from your menu in alphabetical order.

   _____   _____

   _____   _____

   _____   _____

7. Write your own menu item. Include the name, a description, and the price.

   Peanut Butter Cake and Jelly Ice Cream

   _____

   _____

   _____

CREATE YOUR OWN FOOD SPECIALTY

Welcome to the world's first create-it-yourself restaurant. Make your own menu. Any liquid may be served over any solid. Solids may be prepared by any method. May we recommend today's special? It's butterscotch sauce over frozen squash. Use this list of possible preparation methods, liquids, and solids in creating your own food specialties.

Preparation Method	Solids	Liquids
barbecued	squash	French dressing
baked	corn on the cob	milk
pureed	mushrooms	honey
whipped	steak	tartar sauce
raw	fish sticks	butterscotch sauce
chopped	tomato slices	melted butter
boiled	melon balls	coffee
frozen	French fries	maple syrup
grilled	angel food cake	mushroom sauce
dried	brownies	mayonnaise
_____	_____	_____
_____	_____	_____
_____	_____	_____

1. To the list above, add three more preparation methods, three more solids, and three more liquids.

2. Now plan a meal using the directions above. Have at least five specialties to eat. You may use the foods and methods you suggested in answering question 1. Write the menu on a separate sheet.

3. Write down how your favorite food is cooked at home. First list all the ingredients. Then tell how they are put together. How is it cooked and for how long? How is it served? What other foods go with it? If you are not sure of an answer to these questions, make up an answer that sounds believable.

4. Draw a picture of two of the food specialties you have made up.

PIZZA MENU

Name _____

DON'T MISS JOE'S PIZZA ➤

Directions: You will need a pizza menu to do this worksheet.

1. From what restaurant did the menu come? Put the address and phone number below also.

   _____

   _____

2. Which pizza is your favorite? Why? _____

   _____

3. How many different ingredients for pizza does this restaurant offer? List them in alphabetical order on the back of this paper. Don't forget to include tomato sauce and cheese.

4. If you weren't hungry for pizza, is there something else you could order from this restaurant? What would you choose?

   _____

5. You have $10.00 to spend. Write down below what you would order for yourself and a friend.

   You _____ Your friend _____

   How much change would you receive? _____

6. Which pizza is least expensive?   _____

7. Which pizza is most expensive?   _____

8. Make the chart below on the back of this page. Put all the pizzas from your menu on this chart. Put each one under the heading that tells how you feel about it.

   Yum-yum! 😊   Not sure... 😐   No, thanks! 😖
   Love to try it!   Might be good.   Sounds strange to me!

WHAT'S IN THE NEWS?

Obtain the Materials

Most local publishers sell their newspaper for half price for classroom use. They often distribute ideas for using the paper too. For many of the activities which follow, it is not necessary for the children to have the same issue of the newspaper, so obtaining numerous copies from the children themselves should not be difficult. Class members can also bring one-day-old papers if they all need the same issue for small-group work or group sharing activities.

Begin Your Study by Discussing

Without prior study have the children name as many elements of a newspaper as they can. They might mention foreign, national, and local news; columns and editorials; birth and death announcements; comics; advertisements; TV listings; and many others. Now let the students try to locate examples of each by cutting up old newspapers and making a booklet in which they label the illustration of each element.

Word-Recognition Skills

Phonetic Analysis

> Phonetic analysis is the ability to "sound out" or "decode" words by a phoneme–grapheme relationship. These words become part of the sight vocabulary when they can be immediately recognized or instantaneously "sounded out."

☐ Find the Word. Direct the class to circle all words on a specified page of the newspaper that begin or end with a certain sound or blend that you have been studying in class.

☐ Sort the Sound. Instruct the students to make columns on a sheet of paper for each short-vowel sound. Let them conduct a word hunt in the newspaper to find as many words as they can with short-vowel sounds to enter in the appropriate column. This activity can be varied by hunting for long-vowel sounds, digraphs, or diphthongs.

☐ Word Collage. Let the children cut out words they know from the headlines, subheads, or advertisements and paste them on a paper as a collage.

Structural Analysis

> Structural analysis is the habit of recognizing words by the smaller, more meaningful units within the word. Because structural analysis is for the most part a habit, practice is probably the most important key to success. The newspaper can be of the greatest help because the paper can be marked and cut without damage to valuable textbooks or time-consuming, teacher-prepared materials.

☐ Identifying Parts of Words. Select an article containing several multi-syllable words. Then ask the students to practice their structural analysis skills by:
   ▫ Circling compound words.
   ▫ Underlining prefixes and suffixes.
   ▫ Making a slash mark to divide words into syllables.

☐ Headline Cut-Up. Cut out headlines from the paper. Cut the words into syllables, mounting each on separate cards. Use these word parts as practice cards for sounding out, for identifying prefixes and suffixes, and for pointing out how smaller words go into making larger words. (Hint: The students can also combine these parts to make new words. The meanings of the syllables can be written on the back.)

Contextual Analysis

Contextual analysis is the ability to recognize words and their meaning by the function of a word in a familiar sentence pattern.

☐ Guess the Meaning. *Direct the class to read an article in which several new words are found. See if the class can figure out the meaning by the context. Select a student to read the definition aloud from the dictionary to see if the group was correct.*

☐ Word Detective *(also called the Cloze Technique). Pick several ads, the comics, or a simple news story and delete some of the words by covering them with correction fluid or masking tape. Make a duplicator master, and run a copy for each student. The reader simply tries to guess the words that were taken out and then writes them in. This technique is especially recommended for students who decode well but understand little of what they read. It also aids in understanding the patterns of language.*

> If you visit a small town in Japan a week before New Year's, you will find   getting ready for the big celebration. The mothers steam rice in   iron kettles.

☐ Funny News. *Choose a simple story from the newspaper. Underline some of the words or phrases with a lead pencil. Make a duplicator master, and run copies for each student. Then ask the students to substitute their own words or phrases for those that are underlined. Let them be creative and make up a story as different as possible from the original. Let them share their stories with the class.*

rowed

> Sarah and Dave and Josh now pulled their mother into the cabin, and then Dave threw the heavy wooden bar across the door.

wet

Practice with the Newspaper

☐ Good and Bad News. *Have students separate news items into "good news" and "bad news." They can circle the "good news" with red crayon and the "bad news" with blue crayon. Discuss which kind predominates. If the bad news is predominant, let them see if they can explain why.*

☐ Advice Column. *Read a few questions and answers from the advice column in the newspaper. Discuss such issues as: "Do the questions represent common problems?" or "Is the advice given helpful?" Next read a question from the paper, and let the students give their solution to the problem. Pursue this exercise further by letting some students be a Dear Ann or Dear Andy and respond to questions other children have written. This gives them a chance to be witty, sympathetic, outraged, wise, and so on.*

☐ Impromptu Speeches. *Headlines can be clipped and put into a hat. Individuals may draw them as subjects for impromptu speeches.*

☐ Stock Market. *Have each student or group select a stock from the quotations listed in the financial section and record all the information listed (high, low, close). They should continue to record the daily progress of that stock for about three weeks. At the end of that time, complete the following:*

1. *Tell what each of the items you have recorded is and what it means.*

2. *Make a graph showing the rise or decline of the stock over the weeks.*

3. *If you had invested $4,000 in the stock on the first day you selected it, how many shares would you have purchased?*

4. *If you had sold the stock on the last day you recorded it, how much money would you have gained or lost?*

☐ Making History. *Make a bulletin board of what the students think is the most important story each day. At the end of a week or two, discuss which one of these news items will make it into history books.*

☐ Reporting. *A reporter must be a careful observer, have a good memory, be facile with words, and be able to keep his or her wits in a confusing situation. Stage an event in the classroom with another teacher, a parent, or one of your students. During a regular lesson have this person come bursting into the room, pick up some object, and shout a few words like, "I'll get you yet, Batman. I'll never forget what you did to Freddy." Whatever the actor does should be surprising, fast, and loud, but not terrifying (no gunplay). After the actor has gone, have the students write a newspaper account of what took place. Suggest that they include as much detail as they can, describe the setting and appearance of the intruder, and quote what was said. You may wish to let them editorialize and write what they think the intruder's motive was. Let the students compare their write-ups. If some produced highly accurate reports, have them talk about how they felt and reacted during the event.*

- [ ] **Purchasing.** Let the students cut out advertisements of anything they want. Now allow each of them a certain amount of money, and let them pick the things they want most that are within their budget. For variation, use the classified ads.

- [ ] **Classified Ads.** After gaining familiarity with classifieds, students can practice writing ads for themselves. As a first assignment have them each write a four-line ad selling a bicycle or some familiar item. Point out that classified ads are sold by the line and usually have an abundance of abbreviations. A line usually consists of 26 characters (letters, punctuation marks, and spaces). If a line costs $.50, their four-line ad will cost $2.00. Can the student rewrite the ad in three lines? in two? Is the two-line ad weaker than the four-line version? If possible, actually place an ad, and evaluate the results.

- [ ] **Censorship vs. Freedom of the Press.** Freedom of the press, like a lot of other freedoms, is essentially an abstract idea. Some of the implications of censorship can be demonstrated for your students by creating several "censorship boards" in your class. Students will role play special-interest groups—industrialists, unions, ethnic groups, farmers, Democrats, Republicans, and others. Each group will have the right to veto or rewrite any article that it finds damaging or embarrassing to its interests. Now pass out copies of the paper, and let each group find articles they wish to censor. Let the groups come together and discuss the censored and rewritten articles. Then talk about what happens to Mr. or Ms. Average Citizen when the news is adapted for special-interest groups. Is it better for the public to have access to all information? How about construction details of a new secret weapon? a cancer cure that is not yet proven safe? Let the students come up with their own rules about what should be printed.

- [ ] **Headlines.** Pick out several headlines from the paper. Read them to the children one at a time. See if the students can figure out the content of the articles just from the headlines.

- [ ] **Discussion Starters.** Read articles about injustices or social problems to the children. Discuss what solutions can be found to the problems.

- [ ] **Press Conference.** The press conferences on TV have undoubtedly familiarized your students with this phase of newspaper work. Let the students decide who should be interviewed. You might suggest a figure from history, or you might invite a special guest to your class. If you select someone from history, let a child do research in the library and then role play that individual. Questions at a press conference should touch upon feelings as well as facts. Tape record the mock press conference so that the children can analyze their questions. Then they write up the interview giving direct quotations, the guest's opinions, and supporting details. Each write-up should have a suitable headline.

☐ **Editorials.** *Opinions make for some of the liveliest and most provocative writing found in the newspaper. Study editorials and "Letters to the Editor" found in the newspaper. Find an issue that the class is really interested in, like "Should we vote yes on the bond election for city parks?" or "Should wages of policemen be raised?" Instruct them to write an editorial or letter to the editor.*

☐ **Comprehension.** *Read several short articles. As you read each one, have the class make up headlines which express the main idea of the story. Have students read several articles from their newspaper and find the main-idea sentence. (Hint: It will usually be the first sentence.) Let them compare the location of the main-idea sentence in feature stories, front page news stories, and editorials. Ask students to outline feature stories by underlining and numbering key ideas, as in the example below.*

Aquateam Brings U.S.A. Big Swim Win

I   SMITH CITY—While <u>the United States' leadership in speed swimming is</u> constantly <u>threatened</u>, <u>American synchronized swimming has left challengers far behind.</u>

A   Thanks are due mainly to the Smith City Aquateam.

B   The Aquateam won all the gold medals in the World Aquatic Games syncro competition by winning the team event Friday.

C   Aided by two swimmers who were members of the 1976 World Champion team of event winners, the Aquateam presented an exciting routine in which they swam under water in unison for nearly a half-minute.

D   The team was rewarded with a score of 128.64 points, nearly four points ahead of runnerup Canada.

E   Members of the squad were Maria Lopez and Sharon Carroll, both veterans of the 1976 champs; and Lois Phelps, Carla Persutti, Pam Carter, Mazie Jones, Judith Stein, and Meg Castle.

II   When the third World Aquatics Championships were all over, only the United States and East Germany could hold their heads above water.

A   The strong American and East German teams overwhelmed the field, and their only competition was against each other.

B   The United States Friday claimed its second straight World Aquatics Championships team victory, finishing with 16 gold, 11 silver, and 10 bronze medals. East Germany totalled 11 gold, 7 silver and 5 bronze.

C   But the Americans' team total included 3 gold medals won in synchronized swimming and 2 in diving. Without those medals, the two swimming powers each finished with 11 gold, almost exactly where they left off two years ago at the second Aquatic Games in Canada.

Listening Exercises

☐ **What Did You Hear?** *Select a short, interesting article from the newspaper. Read it to the class, asking them to listen for details. Have about five multiple-choice questions on a ditto for them to answer about the article. Correct the questions in class. Ask those who got all the answers correct how they remembered the details. Offer some suggestions of your own on how to increase listening skills. (Hint: Use headline clues, main-idea sentences, vocal stresses, and the five Ws and one H in journalistic reporting listed below.)*

Topic: _____

Answer each of the following question words with information from the article you just heard.

Who?

What?

When?

Where?

Why?

How?

You may wish to pass out to the students copies of the above box. Read an article from the newspaper and let them fill in the facts from the newspaper account.

☐   Distraction. Try an experiment. Have a small part of the class serve as distractors (softly talking, drumming the table with a pencil, walking around, and so on) while the larger part of the class is listening to an article about which they are to answer questions. Discuss the role noise and distraction play in memory.

☐   Newspaper Bingo Game. Select ten words from the headlines on the front page that are suitable for your grade level. Prepare clues for these words which will enable the students to identify them. Read each definition to the class. The children search for the word. When they find it, they circle it and put the number of the clue on it. You may include some words from the subheads, too, in order to increase the difficulty level. The clues might be based on phonics, abbreviations, antonyms, synonyms, compound words, categories, or others you might think of. Some samples are given below:

      ☐ This word is both a girl's name and a legal term. (Sue)

      ☐ This word means "to walk." (stroll)

      ☐ Find three words which have to do with money. (price, wage, bank)

      ☐ This word is made up of two smaller words and means "chase." (manhunt)

      ☐ This word is the opposite of basement. (attic)

      ☐ An abbreviation for the Federal Bureau of Investigation. (FBI)

      ☐ A three-syllable word that means "fuel." (gasoline)

      ☐ The name of one of our states. (Hawaii)

      ☐ A word meaning "two people." (couple)

      ☐ The opposite of "export." (import)

On your paper, write the titles for these three categories: people, places, and things. Find ten words from the newspaper for each category.

People	Places	Things
L. Turner	Kansas	bomb
Sam Smith	Paris	bench

Make up a news article about something that you think could happen. It could be something at home or at school. Make up a headline and draw an illustration for your article.

CAFETERIA SERVES GRAVY

School Held Outside

Students Become Teachers

Make some cut-up sentences using words and phrases that you find in your newspaper. Cut out the words and phrases and paste them on your paper to make three sentences.

The President | met | the Oakland A's.

Moon men | are | in the U.S. Senate.

Look through the comics in your newspaper. Make up your own comic strip. Use some ideas from the comics to help you. In balloons, write the words your characters say.

In the movie section, look through all the ads for movies that are playing. On a piece of paper, write the names of five movies and the theaters where they are playing. Include the movie times if they are in the ad.

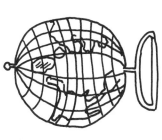

Now Showing:
YOUR FAVORITE MOVIE

Find an article for each of these categories, and write the title and a brief sentence about the article.

Local news:
State news:
National news:
International news:

Look through the sports section. Read three articles, and for each one, list the following:

Name of the sport:

Team names:

Final score:

Something interesting or unusual about the game:

Some writing in the newspaper is _fact_ and some is _opinion_. Write down the titles of four factual articles and four writings that express opinion.

FACTVILLE
Home of all news that is fact

OPINION CITY
Home of all columns, reviews, editorials.

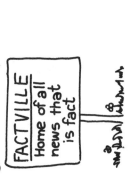

Find ten compound words in your newspaper. Write the words down, and divide them into syllables.

Look through the want-ad section. Find five ads for things you might want to buy. Write those ads on a piece of paper.

Headlines are "catchy phrases" that newspapers use to get you interested in a story. Think of five nursery rhymes or fairy tales. Write an interesting headline for each one.

MYSTERIOUS "GLASS-SLIPPER LADY "FOUND AFTER SEARCH

GOLDILOCKS REPORTED SEEN AGAIN

TWO HURT IN FALL DOWN HILL

Select an interesting article from your newspaper. From the article choose ten words, and write them on your paper. For each word write either a synonym (word that means the same)or antonym (opposite).

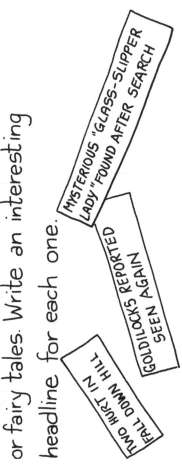

Look in the "help wanted" section of the want-ads. Find a job that would interest you if you were job hunting. Tell what the job is and why you would like it.

39 FLYING LESSONS HERE

Newspapers have several different sections. Write down the names of the sections and the title of one article from each section. Read an article from each section, too.

Editorials

MOVIES-TV

SPORTS

Your six-year-old sister must stay in bed all day with the chicken pox. Look through the television page, and write out a schedule of the programs she would watch all day.

Pretend that you need to sell something in the want-ad section. Write ads for three items. Read over the want-ad section to see how to phrase your ad. Remember to be as brief as possible.

WHAT'S ON TV?

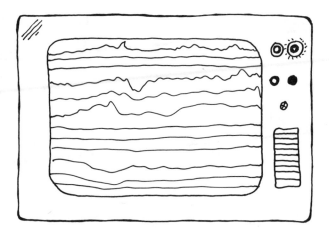

Obtain the Materials

TV Times or TV Guide is available in most homes. Students and fellow teachers would probably be willing to bring in a previous week's copy. The TV guide in the local newspaper can also be used for most of the following activities. Listings for different weeks can add interest and value to the lesson too.

Begin Your Study of the TV Guide by Discussing

☐ Parts of the Guide

- ▫ Cover picture and write-up inside the cover
- ▫ Articles about specific shows or personalities
- ▫ Letters-to-the-editor section
- ▫ Best movies for the week and their ratings
- ▫ Best sports broadcasts for the week
- ▫ Reason for and number of advertisements

☐ Finding Specific Information

    □ *How many different channels are there? How many do you get? Why don't you get them all?*

    □ *What time does the earliest show come on?*

    □ *How late are television shows on?*

    □ *When does Channel (your choice) come on the air?*

    □ *On Wednesday what time does (program of your choice) come on?*

    □ *What comes on after (program of your choice) on Thursday?*

    □ *Skim to find an ad for (product of your choice). What page is the ad on? What is the price?*

Practice with the TV Guide

Research and Math Activities

☐ Charts. *Ask each child to make a chart showing how much time he or she spends watching TV for seven days. Have the children take their charts home and fill in the time slots for each show they watch. Have them add up the total hours of viewing for the week.*

☐ TV Time. *Ask the children to chart a record of how much time the TV set is on during the week in their homes and to add up the total number of hours.*

☐ Violence. *Ask the children to pick out their favorite shows on television and to tally the number of acts of violence they see during each show including:*

    □ *Murders*

    □ *Fights*

    □ *Knockouts*

    □ *Wounds inflicted*

    □ *Crashes*

    □ *Groups wiped out by explosions, wars, or the like*

    □ *Others*

☐ Ad Time. *Ask the children to use a stopwatch or a watch with a second hand to time all the ads during specified shows at different times during the day and to record what show they were watching and the total amount of advertising time. Ask them to consider whether some kinds of shows have more advertising than others.*

☐ Viewing Time. *Ask the children to decide, if each person in the family of four watched TV one hour a day, what the total viewing time for the whole family would be in a week?*

☐ **Air Time.** *Ask the children to find out how many hours Channel (their choice) is on the air on Tuesdays?*

Language Arts Activities

☐ **Programming.** *Divide the class into groups of three or four children. Each group will form a committee to work on one of the following areas of television programming:*
  ▫ *Commercials*
  ▫ *News—sports, weather, on-the-spot*
  ▫ *Documentary*
  ▫ *Coverage of a sports event*
  ▫ *Soap opera*
  ▫ *Talent show or talk show*
  ▫ *Game show—a variation or an original*
  ▫ *Drama or comedy*
  Each group is to create its own production and share it with the rest of the class.

☐ **Ads.** *Ask the child to make a 30-second commercial for a make-believe product. Put it on tape if you wish. Ask the children to make pictures to illustrate it or to pantomime the action.*

☐ **Letters.** *Ask the children to write letters to TV Times asking questions they've been wondering about or to write to the president of one of the major networks to explain their views on programming.*

☐ **Words.** *Ask the children to find three words they don't know in TV Guide and look them up in the dictionary. Ask them to write words in their word notebooks or on a paper to be handed in to you. Ask them to use each word in a sentence.*

☐ **Title.** *Ask each child to think up new titles for three popular TV shows and to write the old title with the new title beside it.*

Name_____

Directions: You will need a TV Guide or the weekly listing of shows from the newspaper to do this worksheet.

1. What is your favorite TV show? List the day, time, and channel.

_____

2. If you could watch television for two hours on Monday, what would you watch?

_____   _____

_____   _____

3. What is your favorite show for each of these days?

Tuesday _____

Thursday _____

Friday _____

Saturday _____

Sunday _____

My Best Show

I LOVE TV

4. Who or what is on the cover of your TV magazine?

_____

5. Choose a movie to watch on Wednesday. Write its title and rating.

_____   _____

6. Choose a game show to watch on Tuesday morning. Write the name and what time the show is on.

_____   _____

7. Choose a cartoon to watch on Saturday morning. Write its name and why you chose it.

_____

LET'S MAKE MUSIC

Begin Your Study by Discussing

Music and rhythm have a universal appeal for children. Every child can join in and participate, no matter what his or her ability level. The lyrics to music stretch the mind and imagination and often contain new language patterns and vocabulary. The two well-known songs included in this section were chosen from the broad spectrum of music from which you can draw to develop reading skills and games. Country and rock music are especially appealing to older children. Sing any song you select for several days in class to become thoroughly familiar with it before you begin your study.

☐ Discuss a Song. *Talk about how the song you choose came to be written, the thoughts that it expresses, who the composer and lyricist are, and how the words and music complement each other.*

☐ Memorize a Song. *The children can either sing or say the song. Memorizing takes discipline and attention to detail. The song selected for each child to learn should be within his or her ability level. Most children find memorizing a successful and satisfying experience.*

☐ The National Anthem. *Give each child a copy of the words to "The Star-Spangled Banner" (see p. 52). Discuss why some of the letters are left out of words in "The Star-Spangled Banner." Note that songs are like poetry and have a certain rhythm and that the number of syllables in the line is very important. Have the students count the number of syllables in each line of the song. Have them clap out the rhythm and explain that the arrows are there to complete the rhythm pattern. Each word with an arrow should be held for two beats.*

Practicing with Music

☐ Song Research. *Assign a different song to each of several committees. In each group, assign some members to do research on the composer and lyricist and history of a song, some to work on illustrations for it, and some to work on recording it.*

☐ Slides. *Make a slide show with a musical accompaniment. Have children draw illustrations for a song on glass or plastic slides and then record their own voices singing. Make sure they work on diction so that the words can be easily understood.*

☐ Words and Music. *Make a study of famous lyricists and composers, and listen to recordings of their compositions.*

☐ Password. *Play Password with the words from a song you have selected. One child sits in front of the class facing the other students. The teacher writes a word from the song on the chalkboard in full view of the class but so that the child who is "It" cannot see it. The object of the game is for "It" to guess the word from one-word clues given by classmates. The pupil who gives the clue which enables "It" to guess correctly becomes "It" next.*

☐ Concentration. *Play Concentration, using words from "The Star-Spangled Banner." On pp. 53 and 54 are the word cards for two games of Concentration—one using words from the first verse of the song and their synonyms and the other using words from the last stanza and their synonyms. Each game includes ten pairs of synonyms. Duplicate the cards on paper heavy enough so that the children cannot see the words through the back. Cut the cards apart. In rows, place each card face down on a table or other playing surface. Two to four children can play. The first player turns up two cards. If the two cards are synonyms, the player keeps them and turns up two more cards, continuing to turn over two cards at a time as long as each pair matches. If the two cards are not synonyms, the player puts them both face down again in the same spot, and play passes to the player to the left. This player repeats the process, trying to remember which words are where, so that he or she can get a match. Continue in this way until all of the cards are picked up. The winner is the player with the most pairs. The game should be played two or three times until all the children know the synonyms. The purpose of this game is to help the children expand their vocabulary by learning the meanings of words in the songs they sing. The children could make up games like this for other songs they sing.*

☐ Crossword. *Do the "America, the Beautiful" crossword puzzle, duplicating copies for the children from the master on pp. 55 and 56.*

THE STAR SPANGLED BANNER

First Verse

Oh→, say, can you see, by the dawn's early light
What so proudly we hailed at the twilight's last gleaming?
Whose broad stripes and bright stars, through the perilous fight,
O'er the ramparts we watched, were so gallantly streaming?
And the rocket's red glare, the bombs bursting in air,
Gave proof through the night that our flag was still there.
Oh, say, does that → star-spangled banner → yet → wave →,
O'er the land → of the free and the home of the brave?

Last Verse

Oh→, thus be it ever, when free men shall stand
Between their loved homes and the war's desolation;
Blest with vict'ry and peace, may the heav'n rescued land
Praise the pow'r that hath made and preserved us a nation!
Then conquer we must, when our cause it is just;
And this be our motto: "In → God is our trust!"
And the star-spangled → banner in triumph → shall → wave →
O'er the land → of the free, and the home of the brave.

Words by Francis Scott Key
Music based on an old English melody

→ : Hold this note for *two* beats as you sing.

desolation	wreckage	rescued	saved
praise	thank	preserved	kept
nation	country	conquer	win
just	fair	motto	saying
wave	fly	triumph	victory

sprinkled	greeted	shining	dangerous	bravely
spangled	hailed	gleaming	perilous	gallantly
flag	sunrise	sunset	wide	protective barrier
banner	dawn	twilight	broad	ramparts

AMERICA, THE BEAUTIFUL

The words in this puzzle are taken from the song with this title. The words marked with a star ★ are the only words that are not found in the first or last verse of the song. If you get stumped, pick out some words in the song that you do not know the meaning of and look them up in the dictionary. Then find a definition that fits from the words below and fill in the word following the appropriate number.

First Verse

O beautiful for spacious skies, for amber waves of grain,
For purple mountain majesties above the fruited plain!
America! America! God shed His grace on thee,
And crown thy good with brotherhood from sea to shining sea!

Last Verse

O beautiful for patriot dream that sees beyond the years,
Thine alabaster cities gleam, undimmed by human tears!
America! America! God shed His grace on thee,
And crown thy good with brotherhood from sea to shining sea!

Across		*Down*	
2.	lovely	1.	grand heights
4.	over	2.	deep concern about others
6.	large, roomy	3.	food-bearing
8.	opposite of "hers"	5.	violet
9.	ocean	7.	heavens
11.	very big hill	10.	white, shiny rock
12.	rippling movements	★11.	I
13.	poured out	★14.	opposite of "she"
14.	of people	16.	level land
15.	your	18.	not dulled
★17.	the answer in an addition problem	★19.	dawn
★20.	opposite of "yes"	21.	gold
22.	one who loves his or her country		
23.	vision		
24.	not out		
25.	farther than		
26.	oats, wheat, barley, and so on		

Words by Katherine Lee Bates
Music by Samuel A. Ward

Name_____

CROSSWORD PUZZLE

WORDS
TO LIVE BY

The lists on page 59 are made up of words and phrases commonly found on signs and directions in our society. It is essential for boys and girls to learn to read these words to assure their own safety, to avoid embarrassment, to be independent, to fill out forms, and to respond correctly in an emergency. Emphasis on words around us in the environment should help students to increase their vocabulary and reading skills, and develop their confidence. The words are divided into three levels of difficulty and a worksheet is given for each. List 1 is the easiest, List 2 is a bit harder, and List 3 is the most difficult.

Begin Your Study By Discussing

Introduce this unit of study by asking the boys and girls if being able to read has ever helped them out of a tight spot. Then let them tell you about the many times every day that they must read important things outside of school. Ask them to think of important words and phrases that they might find on directions and signs that they should know. Compile a list on the blackboard. This list may become the core for this unit, or you may wish to use the lists that have been provided.

Practicing with Words to Live By

- Have students look in magazines and newspapers for signs, labels, and instructions which one would see frequently. They may make a collage of these words, phrases, or sentences, or they may fold a large piece of newsprint into 12 sections and put one in each section. To be most effective this activity could be done in committees. Each group would divide the words into categories (people, safety, words on buildings, instructions, transportation words or phrases, and so on). Then, for each category, the committee could make up questions to ask the rest of the class.

- Use the words for flashcard games or put them on cards for open-ended game boards.

- Give each child a list of words appropriate to his or her reading ability. Give phonetic clues ("Who can find a word with a silent gh?" or "Who sees a word where the c has the soft sound?"); structural analysis clues ("Can you find a two-syllable word?" or "What is the word that has a prefix?"); or comprehension clues ("What is another word for man?" or "What phrase means you can't go in?"). The children may answer either orally or on paper.

- Use the words as bonus spelling words, handwriting practice, or practice in alphabetizing.

- To assure that children know the meanings of the words, they may illustrate them, pantomime them, or paraphrase them.

- A good homework assignment: Ask the children to look around them and come back to school with as many words as they can find that came off signs or directions.

- Put the words on cards, and let the children draw out three cards apiece. For a unique creative writing assignment have them weave these three words and phrases into a meaningful story. Be sure to share the best efforts with the entire class.

- Let the boys and girls practice reading these words to a partner or cross-age tutor.

- The worksheets on pp. 60 and 61 are samples of activities which you may wish to make up for the other lists.

words to Live by

LIST 2

Beware of Dog	Taxi
Adults Only	Use Before _(date)_
Elevator	Hospital Zone
Do Not Use Near Heat	MPH
Fasten Seat Belt	COD
Entrance	Not a Through Street
Fire Escape	Railroad Crossing
Information	Restrooms
No Trespassing	Yield
Out of Order	Perishable
Poison	Unloading Zone
Private Property	Net Wt.

LIST 1

Bus Stop	City
Deep Water	Closed
Don't Walk	Dentist
Doctor	Do Not Enter
First Aid	Exit
Keep Away	Help
Ladies	No Diving
Gentlemen	Nurse
Men	Police
Women	Push
No Smoking	Pull
Office	Dead End
Post Office	Telephone
Wet Paint	Zip Code
School Zone	State
Area Code	Bus Station
Address	

LIST 3

Antidote	Violators Will Be Prosecuted
Caution	Ask Attendant for Key
Combustible	Detour
High Voltage	Emergency Vehicles Only
Do Not Refreeze	Merging Traffic
Emergency Exit	Pedestrian Xing
Employees Only	Proceed at Your Own Risk
External Use Only	Truck Route
Fire Extinguisher	Cashier
No Admittance	Manual Control
Pedestrians Prohibited	Automatic Control
Smoking Prohibited	Machine Washable

Name _____

ODD ONE OUT

Directions: In each numbered group of three words or phrases from List 1, one word or phrase doesn't belong. Can you find the "odd" word or phrase in each group? Draw a circle around it.

1.	Deep Water	No Diving	(Doctor)
2.	Dead End	Dentist	Nurse
3.	Office	Post Office	Keep Away
4.	Gentlemen	School Zone	Ladies
5.	Exit	First Aid	Nurse
6.	Doctor	Closed	Nurse
7.	Wet Paint	Keep Away	Address
8.	State	Women	City
9.	Zip Code	Area Code	Bus Stop
10.	No Smoking	Telephone	Address
11.	Police	Exit	Do Not Enter
12.	Push	School Zone	Pull
13.	Gentlemen	Women	Ladies
14.	Dead End	Bus Stop	School Zone
15.	Keep Away	Do Not Enter	Telephone
16.	Post Office	Bus Stop	Bus Station

Then choose three of the phrases or words on this page that you feel are most important. Write down a reason for each of your choices.

1. _____

2. _____

3. _____

Name _____

LET'S SOLVE A PROBLEM

What sign or label would you look for in the following situations? Look at the words and phrases in List 2 and write down the one that provides an answer to your question.

1. This bread feels stale. I wonder how old it is? _____

2. How can I go up to the fourth floor? _____

3. I smell smoke. How do I get out of here?_____

4. Those little children drank some of this. Will it hurt them? _____

5. Is this soft drink machine working? _____

6. Is it all right to walk through this field? _____

7. Is this field part of the park, or does it belong to someone? _____

8. Where's the bathroom? _____

9. Do we have to let the other cars go by first?_____

10. Where do we go in? _____

11. Do we have to buckle up? _____

12. This shopping center is so big. Where can I find that coin shop?_____

13. Don't you think that dog is friendly? _____

14. This is not a street. Why does the bus driver stop and look both ways here? _____

15. How can we get home from the airport?_____

16. Why do I have to pay for this package which came in the mail? _____

17. Do I have to keep this in the refrigerator? _____

18. Should I put this gasoline over by the heater? _____

CATEGORIES

Fill in the spaces below with words or phrases from List 3 which fit under the headings.

Signs on Food and Containers

1. _____   4. _____

2. _____   5. _____

3. _____   6. _____

Signs on Doors

1. _____

2. _____

3. _____

4. _____

Signs by the Road

1. _____   5. _____

2. _____   6. _____

3. _____   7. _____

4. _____   8. _____

Make a picture showing where each of the following words or phrases might be used.

1. High Voltage   5. Caution
2. Smoking Prohibited   6. Pedestrians Prohibited
3. Violators Will Be Prosecuted 7. Cashier
4. Proceed at Your Own Risk   8. Merging Traffic

SCHOOL MENUS

Obtain the Materials

School cafeteria menus are usually passed out once a month. If you can arrange to get the menus a day or two early, you could use them for a few days for special activities. Mount extra menus on cardboard or staple them into folders so they will be convenient and durable for additional classroom assignments. Perhaps a fellow teacher from a neighboring district could save some cafeteria menus for comparison with yours. The worksheets in this section can be easily adapted to use with your own school menu.

Begin Your Study by Discussing

Give students an opportunity to read over their menus. You may need to list some of the unfamiliar words on the board (enchilada, ravioli, or the like). Discuss the format of the menu (no Saturday and Sunday), and note the type of food that is featured (appealing to children, balanced meal each day).

Practicing With School Menus

☐ The School Cook. *If possible, invite your school cook in to meet with the class and discuss his or her job. The cook may want to share a recipe or some of the utensils or ingredients used in the cafeteria (large pots, cooking forks, large cans of tomato sauce, or the like).*

☐ The School Kitchen. *A mini-field trip to your school kitchen will heighten interest in and motivation for the menu study. Students will enjoy actually observing the quantities prepared and the large ovens, mixers, warming trays, refrigerators, and so on. The visit could include a short talk about how the food gets to the school, how it is paid for, how the menu is planned, and how the kitchen is kept clean.*

Dear Parents,

Each month we will be sending home a menu from our school's hot lunch program. This menu provides an excellent reading opportunity for your son or daughter. Its content is both interesting and relevant, and it provides a practical application of the reading skills your child is learning each day at school.

You may want to keep the menu in a special place so that you can refer to it during the month. Encourage your child to read the menu, and ask questions about its content, such as:

"What dessert are they serving tomorrow?"
"Which is your favorite lunch for this week?"

In the space below, your child has copied his or her favorite hot lunch from this month's menu.

_____

_____

_____

_____

Thank you for your interest and cooperation.

Sincerely,

UNIFIED SCHOOL DISTRICT

FOOD SERVICES

Student Lunch with Milk   60¢
Additional Milk   15¢
Adult Lunch   90¢

NOVEMBER   1
Hot Dog on a Bun
Potato Pennies
Celery Sticks
Milk
Chilled Pears
Cookie
	2
	Toasted Cheese
	  Sandwich
	Crisp Carrot Sticks
	Milk
	Ambrosia
	Cookie
		3
		Enchilada with Sauce
		  and Cheese
		Buttered Green Peas
		Vegetable Salad
		Milk
		Coffee Cake
		Apple Slices
			4
			Pizza
			Vegetable Relishes
			Milk
			Orange Smiles
			Cookie

8 Chicken Fried Steak Fluffy Whipped Potatoes & Gravy Applesauce Celery Sticks Gingerbread Milk	9 Beef-Filled Ravioli with Sauce, Cheese Peas Chilled Fruit Milk Coffee Cake	10 Golden Browned Fish Warm Roll Tossed Salad Carrot Sticks Milk Fruit Crisp	11 HOLIDAY !

15
Italian Spaghetti
Tossed Green Salad
French Bread
Milk
Chilled Fruit
Chocolate Cake
	16
	Hot Dog on a Bun
	Pork and Beans
	Celery Sticks
	Milk
	Apple Wedges
	Cookie
		17
		THANKSGIVING
		  LUNCH
		Turkey with Bread
		Dressing and Gravy
		Buttered Green Beans
		Milk
		Holiday Vegetable
		  Relishes
		Holiday Pie
			18
			Barbequed Beef
			  on a Bun
			Potato Triangle
			Orange Wedges
			Milk
			Vegetable Salad
			Cookie

22 Cook's Choice	23 Pizza on a Bun Tossed Green Salad Milk Chilled Fruit Cookie	24 HOLIDAY !	25 HOLIDAY

7
Sloppy Joe on a Bun
Green Beans with
  Peanuts
Milk
Shredded Lettuce with
  1,000 Island
  Dressing
Chilled Fruit & Cookie
	14
	Pizza
	Shredded Lettuce
	with French Dressing
	Chilled Fruit
	Milk
	Peanut Butter Cookie
		21
		Beef & Bean Burrito
		Beautiful Buttered
		  Green Peas
		Carrot Sticks
		Applesauce
		Milk
		Gingerbread
			HALLOWEEN
			Spooky Spaghetti
			Broomstick Carrots
			Slice-of-the-Moon
			  Bread
			Witches Brew
			Orange Moon Slices
			Midnight Cake

SCHOOL MENU WORKSHEET 1

You will need a copy of a school menu to do this worksheet.

1. Write down three vegetables, three fruits, and three desserts that are being offered this month.

   _____   _____   _____

   _____   _____   _____

   _____   _____   _____

2. Find at least five adjectives (words that describe) on your menu.

   _____   _____   _____

   _____   _____

3. Choose three entrees that you would like to eat.

   _____   _____   _____

4. Pretend you are the cook and plan a lunch for your school. (Be sure it is a balanced meal.)

   _____   _____

   _____   _____

   _____   _____

   _____   _____

5. Do one of the following on the back of this worksheet:

   A. Draw a picture of the lunch you planned above. Label each item in your picture.

   B. Write about your life as a peanut butter cookie or a vegetable salad.

   C. Conduct a survey with at least ten classmates to determine the five most popular items on the menu.

6. Look on your menu and find a word for each letter of the alphabet. (A = applesauce; B = buttered; C = cake; and so on). Write these words in alphabetical order on the back of this worksheet. Are there some letters which have *no* words?

Name _____

SCHOOL MENU WORKSHEET 2

You will need a copy of the Unified School District menu to do this worksheet.

1. What is the menu for _____ (date)? Circle your favorite item.

   _____   _____

   _____   _____

   _____   _____

2. How many lunches have a cookie? _____

   How many have chilled fruit? _____

3. If three teachers bought their lunches, how much would the total cost be? _____

4. List four foods from this menu that you might also find in another country.

   _____   _____

   _____   _____

5. Can you find the following kinds of words on this menu? Write them on the space provided.

   Short-vowel word _____   One-syllable word _____

   Long-vowel word _____   Two-syllable word _____

   Word with a silent letter _____   Three-syllable word _____

6. Find something on the menu that might be:

   Sweet _____   Juicy _____

   Crunchy _____   Spicy _____

7. What do you think "Cook's Choice" means? If you were the cook, what foods would you offer the students?

   _____   _____

   _____   _____